The Plot

The Plot

Designing Diversity in the Built Environment:
a manual for architects and urban designers

Jonathan Tarbatt

RIBA ✳ Publishing

Published by RIBA Publishing, 15 Bonhill Street,
London EC2P 2EA

ISBN 978 1 85946 443 4

Stock code 77527

British Library Cataloguing in Publication Data
A catalogue record for this book is available from the
British Library.

Designed and typeset by Ashley Western

Printed and bound in Great Britain by W & G Baird Ltd

While every effort has been made to check the accuracy and
quality of the information given in this publication, neither
the Author nor the Publisher accepts any responsibility for
the subsequent use of this information, for any errors or
omissions that it may contain, or for any misunderstandings
arising from it.

RIBA Publishing is part of RIBA Enterprises Ltd.
www.ribaenterprises.com

ii (*left to right from top*):
Loci; City of Almere/John Lewis Marshall; Loci; Loci/Conor Norton;
Arkitema Architects; ANA Architecten; City of Almere/Martijn Steiner Lovisa;
Loci/Jonathan Tarbatt; Loci/Jonathan Tarbatt; Loci/Jonathan Tarbatt;
Jonathan Tarbatt; Loci/Jonathan Tarbatt; Loci/Jonathan Tarbatt;
Tübingen project development department/MANFRED GROHE;
Arkitema Architects; Siebe Swart Photography

v
City of Almere/Top Shot

Acknowledgements

This book is the product of many years interest in diversity
in the built environment. It has been sustained by design-
based research and first-hand experience of co-housing and
self-build projects in the UK and Ireland; numerous field
trips to exemplary projects in France, Germany, Sweden,
Finland and the Netherlands; and the experience gained
bringing this knowledge to bear in my own projects. As a
result, I have benefited from the advice and insight of many
people along the way – clients, practitioners and colleagues
– who are too numerous to mention here.

I am very grateful to all of the practices and individuals who
kindly contributed information and images of their work:
Holger Dahl and Arkitema Architects; Jacqueline Tellinga,
Lydia de Leng-van der Poel and Karen Heijne of Almere
Municipal Authority; Anna Hakkens and Jannie Vinke of ANA
Architects; Cie Architects; Dublin City Library and Archive;
Isaac Lawless; MVRDV; Ordnance Survey Ireland; Porphyrios
Associates; Roger Evans of Studio REAL; Jakub Szczęsny;
Berenice Felsenburg and Selina Heinrich of the Tübingen
Südstadt Municipal Authority (Project Development
Department); Allard Terwel and West 8 Urban Design and
Landscape Architecture; Urban Splash; and of course my
own practice, Loci.

I am especially grateful to RIBA commissioning editor
Matthew Thompson, development editor Sharon Hodgson
and production director Kate Mackillop, for their enthusiasm
and patience; to my parents for their unstinting support and
encouragement; and last but not least, to Chloe Street for
her thoughtful advice and input.

contents

1 Introducing the plot

This book is a manual for making better places: places that are more socially mixed, with more mixed uses and more variety in the design and age of buildings. Dissecting the existing body of official or influential urban design guidance, and examining case examples, it identifies a link between two dominant factors that are instrumental in achieving these goals. The first is the plot, which should be thought of as the basic unit of urban development. The second is diversity of architectural form, which is its key physical characteristic, manifested in mixed-use, close- and medium-grain neighbourhoods.

Close-grain street buildings and townhouses are human in scale and produce more entrances onto the street than do other building typologies. Consequently, they can also serve to enclose and *activate* streets as *places* rather than mere conduits for movement. Their proximity to each other also facilitates the creation of more walkable and healthy neighbourhoods that are less dependent on car transport than those comprising other building types.

The conditions that generated close-grain development in older streets and town centres have changed, however, and in many places this older pattern of development has slid into obsolescence. Often it has been replaced by single-use developments on larger sites, often outside established centres. This trend can be observed throughout the UK and Ireland. It is caused by a variety of interrelated factors, notably property market preferences that favour single-use developments on large plots on the one hand and demand for suburban houses with gardens on the other. As a result of these and related processes, we have lost, or are in the process of losing, the plot, as well as the rich tapestry of urban fabric it supports. Many observers have blamed this for contributing to the economic, social and physical decline of the high street, as well as the poor quality and homogeneity of suburban areas.

The policy concern with making more sustainable places and communities kick-started by the Urban Renaissance in the UK has been tempered by the realisation that existing approaches to place-making have failed, by and large, to create successful places.[1] This has led to a renewed interest in close-grain building typologies, and in the potential of plot-based urbanism to address these core concerns. Vertical mixed-use street buildings, townhouses, apartments and other building typologies laid out on individual small plots are now seen as offering a viable alternative to larger, single-use blocks, as well as a more inherently robust building form and a 'plot-up' approach to regeneration that is more resilient to economic uncertainty.

The book explains how the plot generates diversity of architectural form in the built environment and how designers can exploit plot-based urbanism to help make new places that are more environmentally, economically and socially sustainable. Set in the context of national planning policy, existing regulations, financial considerations, known development models and commercial realities, it goes on to extract broad strategic design parameters for the masterplanner. The objectives are several-fold. They include:

☐ how to create diversity of architectural form at a human scale

☐ how to create places that are more adaptable to change and more resilient to recession than prevailing models of development

☐ how to facilitate engagement in the design and development process by a wide range of designers and developers.

While diversity of architectural form can't *by itself* produce *socio-economic* diversity – which is recognised as being at the heart of sustainable communities – it can create the urban conditions necessary to support it. Understanding of how plot-based urbanism can contribute to this will provide designers, developers and their clients with a competitive

△ Traditional mixed-use street with close-
grain plots, Ballinrobe, County Mayo

edge. This is because support for development proposals, whether in the form of public investment in reinforcing infra-structure or in the public realm, or merely gaining consent, is increasingly dependent on demonstrating how they can achieve these aims.[2]

This book tells you how.

1.1 THE PLOT: DESIGNING DIVERSITY

Successful places – streets, spaces, villages, towns and cities – tend to have certain characteristics in common, and urban designers aim to replicate these characteristics in new development.[3] This book explores the interrelationship between the density and pattern of plot subdivisions – urban grain – and one of the most important, yet elusive, of these characteristics, which is diversity.[4]

Diversity in sucessful places manifests itself in different ways, to different extents and at different scales. Variety of building forms, architectural design and age of buildings, mixed housing types, sizes and tenures, and a mix and intensity of uses, combine to sustain a wide range of activities in close proximity to each other, imparting to each place its own unique character and identity and its sense of place.

The close-grain diversity of mixed-use streets in traditional town centres has been identified by successive studies[5] as epitomising several of the characteristics that urban design tries to capture.[6] One such study, published by the Joseph Rowntree Foundation,[7] summarises the benefits as:

☐ environmental – facilitating people to shop locally without cars

☐ economic – providing a well-connected catchment of customers for local businesses

☐ social – providing inclusive places for local communities to participate in different activities and to meet one another

☐ liveability – creating pleasant and stimulating places for people to pass through and visit.

Taken together, these are essential components of sustainable places and of sustainable communities. But close-grain street buildings are a legacy of an older mode of development that has been rendered obsolete by the market's preference to supply larger (medium- or coarse-grain) single-use developments in town centres, combined with a marked preference on the part of most house buyers to choose detached houses in the suburbs.

The seminal report of the government's Urban Task Force, *Towards an Urban Renaissance*, in 1999 and numerous 'spin-off' urban design manuals such as the *Urban Design Compendium* have documented how the rich urban tradition of town centres 'has yielded to banal and monotonous single-use developments, "humdrum" in design and dominated by traffic. We have repeated standard housing types and layouts, retail boxes and road layouts so many times, with little or no regard for local context, until we find that now almost everywhere looks like everywhere else.'[8]

We are no longer a nation of shopkeepers, however, and any latent demand for living over the shop can be absorbed by the existing stock of older street buildings. Meanwhile, some places that are characterised by close-grain buildings that were once thriving are either in decline or needing comprehensive regeneration. Clearly there are other factors influencing the success or otherwise of urban areas characterised by close-grain plots that need to be understood. The

Losing the plot in the City of London.

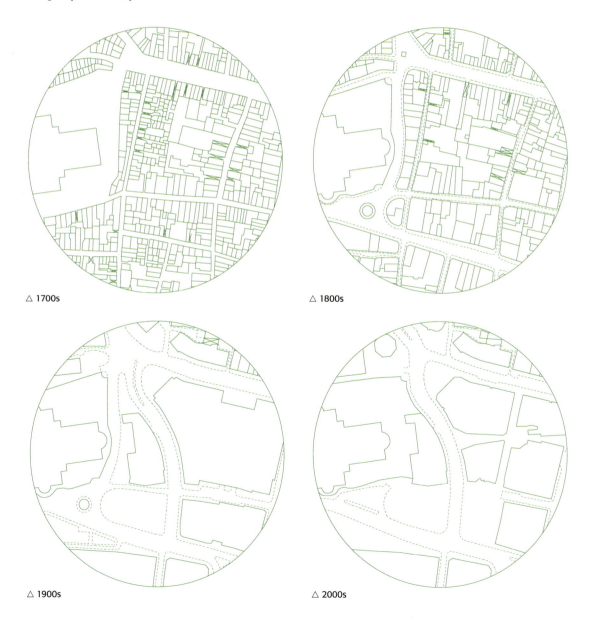

△ 1700s

△ 1800s

△ 1900s

△ 2000s

Joseph Rowntree Foundation, for example, highlights the way in which their success can be hampered by the priority afforded to through traffic over the needs of people who visit them as places in their own right, changes in shopping behaviour and a policy vacuum.[9]

The consequences of the prevailing market-led approach, however, are increasingly acknowledged – by practitioners, policymakers and observers – to be contributing to the stagnation of both town centres *and* the suburbs, giving rise to calls for a more plan-led approach that can overcome negative market perceptions.

Urban designers can strongly influence physical aspects of the built environment for the better – for example, by guiding the scale, height and massing of buildings and building lines. But they are less well placed to deliver those seemingly more intangible aspects – vital communities and thriving local economies – that make those places successful.

And although urban design guidance recognises both the legacy that close urban grain has imparted to the character of traditional town centres and the importance of diversity in making successful places, it has tended to overlook how either can be factored into the design of new places. Much less has it considered how they are, in fact, inextricably linked, or how design strategies can reinforce this link.

This book argues that close urban grain carries with it the DNA of urban form that can foster diversity, support local economies and facilitate a range of alternative development models that can support the creation of more sustainable places. It describes how contiguous plots joined together are the invisible substrate of urban form and how the individual street buildings that occupy them offer the potential to support and foster diversity in all its forms – diversity of design and of uses, urban form, density, housing types, sizes and tenures, and community services – with the potential to generate a synergy of visual, physical, social and economic interrelationships that is greater than the sum of its parts.

It sets out strategic approaches to the design and layout of plots in relation to each other that have the potential to foster diversity. These are based on the simple premise, observed by a range of studies and urban design guidance, that smaller plot subdivisions facilitate greater diversity, and thereby help to create more successful places and more sustainable communities.

Getting the right balance of uses, urban form, density, housing types, sizes and tenures, and community services, however, requires a holistic attention to design at every level. The laying out of smaller plots in relation to each other so as to define compact and walkable streets and spaces, with as diverse a range of compatible activities and uses as it is possible to accommodate, it is argued, is the key to achieving this vision.

1.2 THE DIVERSITY AGENDA: WHY IT'S IMPORTANT

Diversity, in the broadest sense of the word, resonates with the western ideal of a meritocracy: where equality of opportunity, irrespective of age, gender, race, religion or socio-economic background, is seen as democracy in action. Underlying this utopian ideal is a belief that the mixing of people promotes mutual understanding and tolerance. The city itself is valued as a locus of difference: a 'melting pot' for different cultures and lifestyles that generates vital places and enriches human experience.

The ideal of a meritocracy values individuality, and increasingly people want to express their individuality through the design of their homes and workplaces. In the public realm, people from diverse backgrounds can come together and observe each other, occupying the same space on equal terms.

Jane Jacobs's influential book *The Death and Life of Great American Cities* describes how close-grain diversity is both a goal and a marker for how successful places are, measured in terms of the degree to which they exhibit variety, choice and interest: increasing social and economic exchange possibilities in complex 'pools of use'.[10] The core of Jacobs's argument revolves around the idea that the close proximity of different building typologies and uses can create a neighbourhood that provides constant mutual support for its inhabitants, and helps to build social capital by widening networks for social interaction.

More recent research by Talen demonstrates that a range of plot sizes is an indicator of places that are more socially diverse, because it allows a wider range of entrants to the property market.[11] Places characterised by a diverse range of close-grain uses are also seen as being more responsive to change and more resilient to economic downturn. If an area has developed piecemeal from small parts, then no single part is 'too big to fail', and robustness is 'built in' to the urban fabric.

In the UK and Ireland mixed housing tenures and mixed uses are now seen by policymakers and urban designers alike as vital features of successful places and sustainable communities that need to be preserved. They are also a 'must have' in stimulating an urban renaissance, to which people are 'drawn by a lifestyle where home, work and leisure are interwoven within a single neighbourhood'.[12]

Where once planning sought to solve urban problems by segregating them – segregating people from cars, segregating places for living from places for working, and segregating the 'haves' from the 'have-nots' – now its opposite, diversity, is seen as part of the solution, and design as one way of delivering it. There is a drive towards the creation of more compact and diverse urban settlement patterns in new places and towards the repair of suburban ones. Likewise, there is increasing acceptance that in more financially straitened times low-key 'plot-up' approaches to the regeneration of older urban settlements are likely to become more relevant than ever before.

1.3 POLICY AND PRACTICE: THE CHALLENGE FOR DESIGNERS

The overarching goal of successive iterations of government policy on architecture and the built environment is to create sustainable communities:

> Places where people want to live and work, now and in the future. They meet the diverse needs of existing and future residents, are sensitive to their environment, and contribute to a high quality of life. They are safe and inclusive, well planned, built and run, and offer equality of opportunity and good services for all.[13]

Urban design is now more than ever concerned with acting as coordinator, integrator and mediator of the spatial dimensions of a wide range of policy streams and the close-grain mixed-use street is rising in importance on the UK government's policy agenda, as it has the potential to address these interrelated policy concerns.[14]

The National Planning Policy Framework (for England) urges local planning authorities to foster sustainable communities by devising 'policies which promote opportunities for meetings between members of the community who might not otherwise come into contact with each other, including through mixed-use developments, strong neighbourhood centres and active street frontages which bring together those who work, live and play in the vicinity'.[15]

The principal urban design guidance document in the UK, *By Design: Urban Design in the planning system*, identifies a wide range of characteristics – character, continuity and enclosure, quality public realm, ease of movement, legibility, adaptability and diversity – and their implications for urban form, which it seeks to combine in order to create frameworks for development.[16] In doing so it draws together different strands of place-making, such as town planning, architecture, development economics, and environmental

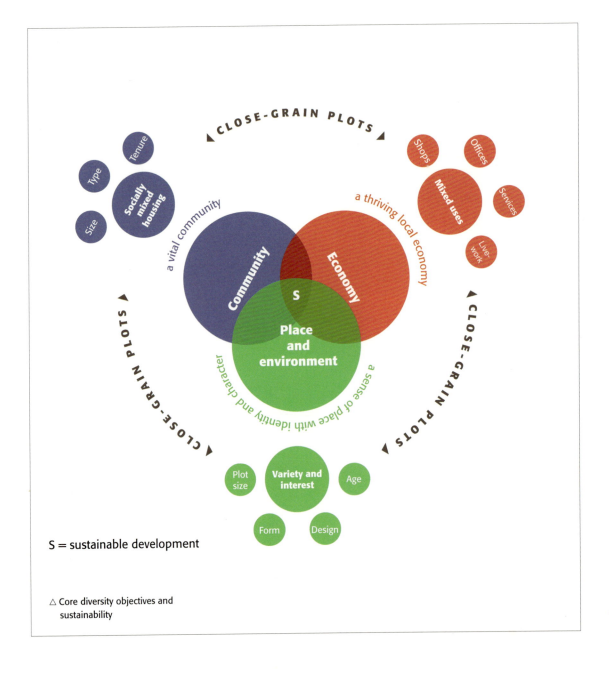

S = sustainable development

△ Core diversity objectives and
  sustainability

and social considerations, while at the same time transcending them, to create places in which diverse communities can flourish.[17]

Supporting best practice, urban design guidelines such as the *Urban Design Compendium* acknowledge the benefits of close-grain diversity, but practice has focused on more readily achievable outcomes – a return to more compact and permeable urban frameworks – without planning for plots. As a result, the ambition to achieve coherence without conformity has not been matched by achievement.[18]

In line with the diversity agenda, urban design guidance promotes the importance of achieving (and retaining) diversity of uses and variety of architectural expression, and masterplans themselves are increasingly seeking (or expected) to include close-grain and/or mixed-grain development as a requirement rather than merely a preference. Schemes are increasingly judged by local authority and funding agencies against how well they achieve these sorts of urban design criteria, and the results can and do influence whether a scheme will achieve public funding support and how smoothly it can progress through the system.

Caution is warranted, however, because greater intensity of uses can lead to gentrification, pricing local people out of their own neighbourhood, or the creation of enclaves that are more, not less, segregated, and because goals of economic regeneration are not the same goals as social equity. Social mixing can reduce cohesion and lead to friction between individuals and community groups, and variety itself can be superficial.

In residential areas, privacy may be of more concern to people than the goals of social inclusion, and even in the high street people may prefer to move about in relative anonymity, making only guarded contact with strangers. As pointed out in the *Urban Design Compendium*, diversity inevitably brings some conflict.

These counterarguments do not present a reason to abandon the goal but a reason to take a more responsive approach to design. The closer we are together, for example, the greater the need for the spaces between us – the public realm and community infrastructure – to be of the highest quality, and the greater the need for diversity to be managed. While many suburbs are successful places in their own right (and clearly people are attracted to live in them), it must be realised that this 'silent majority' hasn't, in general, ever been provided with a more attractive alternative.

Well-designed suburbs are the exception that proves the rule, and more considered masterplanning approaches that provide for close-grain diversity are demonstrating that 'new suburbs' can be developed to a much higher standard of design as well as providing for mixed uses, live-work, affordability, greater adaptability, safety and variety and healthier, more connected pathways for social and community interaction, without making people feel so close together that they are uncomfortable, or that their children don't have enough room to grow.

Just as bad planning and design can lead to the creation of bad places, characterised by homogeneity, segregation, social exclusion and vandalism, good planning and design can produce good places, characterised by diversity, variety, social inclusion, safety and choice. Where one speaks of doubt and a lack of ambition, the other speaks of hope and a belief that good design can make a difference.

The challenge for designers is to respond appropriately to the new policy agenda. The relevance of close- and mixed-grain urban typologies needs to be understood; planning for plots needs to be relearned and the plot reinvented to meet modern needs and expectations.

2 Understanding the plot

2.1   THE PLOT IN URBAN DESIGN THEORY AND PRACTICE

Urban design is defined in *By Design* as the art of making places for people:

> It includes the way places work and matters such as community safety, as well as how they look. It concerns the connections between people and places, movement and urban form, nature and the built fabric, and the processes for ensuring successful villages, towns and cities.[19]

In contrast to urban design, architecture is focused on the design of buildings (and architects are rarely afforded the opportunity to operate beyond the site), whereas town planning is focused on the functions and land uses of larger urban areas (often at the regional level). Urban design operates at the intersections between these two spheres of influence and, as a result, has appropriated the shaping of space *between* buildings as its core concern. The contemporary practice of urban design has thus emerged to fill a vacuum between architecture and town planning.

Urban design recognises, however, that streets and spaces cannot be understood satisfactorily in isolation from the buildings that enclose them and, in turn, from the uses that occupy those buildings. In this sense, urban design is intimately concerned with the interface between *groups* of buildings, their uses *and* public spaces. It overlaps with the traditional domains of architecture and planning with the intention of putting in place the three-dimensional design frameworks within which these and related disciplines (such as urban and economic geography, engineering, transport planning) can be brought together to create successful places.

It is beyond the scope of this book to provide a comprehensive account of urban design theory or practice. Much of the theoretical debate, however, arises from the contrast between evolutionary approaches to urban design that celebrate the emergence of places incrementally, and approaches that promote an idealised blueprint for what a place should be like when it's 'finished'.

Arguably the most influential advocate of evolutionary approaches is Christopher Alexander. His *New Theory of Urban Design*, for example (published in 1987), sets out 'rules' for growing organic 'wholeness' in new urban areas that he contends will generate the same qualities of organic wholeness experienced in traditional towns.[20] He contrasts the piecemeal growth characteristic of traditional towns with modern 'plan-led' practices that he says force an artificial, contrived kind of wholeness. Alexander's first rule establishes the piecemeal character of growth as a precondition of organic wholeness. This, he argues, ensures that the grain of development is small enough for wholeness to develop. Crucially, he supplements the rule with a sub-rule relating to the distribution of different land uses in the piecemeal growth.

Alexander is quick to acknowledge, however, that piecemeal growth by itself can lead to chaos if it is not structured in some way. But he rejects the role of the plan in providing this structure on the basis that plans create order without organic feeling. Accordingly, Alexander's second rule posits that every act of incremental building must contribute to a larger whole. Alexander's team conducted a series of experiments to test their rules, but they found that attempting to structure urban growth in this way tended to produce urban form that was piecemeal in the bad sense, because it produced fragmented aggregations rather than coherent wholes.

Evolutionary approaches to urban design contrast with more systematic approaches, which rely on the production of an overarching 'plan'. Masterplanning is one of the principal urban design activities engaged in by urban designers and architects alike, and plan-led approaches are embedded in nearly all contemporary urban design guidance.

According to the Commission for Architecture and the Built Environment (CABE [now Design Council/CABE]), the widespread practice of masterplanning has emerged in response to the need to set frameworks within which change at a large scale can be managed, allowing multiple development proposals to be brought forward in a planned and coordinated way.[21] As such, the term implies a larger scale of intervention but a reduced level of detail than is commonly associated with site layout planning for individual sites. Other terms in common usage include 'urban design frameworks' and 'development frameworks', which amount to the same thing. CABE thus defines masterplanning as both a *process*, by which organisations prepare analyses and develop strategies for development, and a *product*, which sets out proposals for a specific area of land for land uses, movement, buildings and spaces in three dimensions.[22]

Masterplans are often supplemented by a more detailed set of design guidance in the form of a design code, commonly organised around the different street typologies identified in the masterplan. The Department for Communities and Local Government's guidance for the preparation of design codes defines them as 'a set of written and graphic rules that establish with precision the two and three dimensional design elements of a particular development or area – and how these relate to one another without establishing the overall outcome'.[23] The aim of design codes is to provide clarity over what constitutes acceptable design quality for a particular site or area.[24] However, they are frequently criticised on the grounds that too much prescription tends to stifle creativity and to result in formulaic solutions.

The contrast in both timescale and scale of operation of urban design and planning compared with architecture brings to light a key source of tension between them. Whereas architecture is concerned with the production of a specific building or buildings within a set period of time (and designed by a specific practice), urban design and planning are more concerned with the ongoing process of placemaking over a much longer period of time, which doesn't have a predetermined outcome.

The issue with masterplans, by extension, is that they often give the misleading impression of a place as an 'end product' rather than something that is created and changed by the ongoing interaction of many complex processes and agents. This issue is compounded when architects are permitted, or even encouraged, to design entire urban areas by themselves, because their inclination to treat the plan as a single project involving the procurement of a collection of buildings inadvertently inhibits the potential for diversity and variety that occurs over time in places that have grown and changed incrementally. Campbell argues that this preoccupation of architects with 'product' is harming architecture and, by extension, urbanism, because at the urban scale design cannot be the singular vision of the lone architect, and thus cannot be based on a conventional architectural approach extended to the city scale.[25]

Suffice to say that contemporary masterplanning practice has not, by and large, produced successful places, yet truly evolutionary approaches cannot hope to be replicated under current conditions. A middle ground needs to be found, and it is argued that the plot is the key to bridging this gap.

The approach described in this book – loosely referred to as 'plot-based urbanism' – tries to reconcile the divergent agendas of evolutionary and plan-led approaches to urban design by reintroducing close-grain and mixed-grain plot typologies within a masterplanning framework. It promotes the benefits of incrementalism inherent in plot-based urbanism, while facilitating the preference of the development industry and contemporary urban design practice to promote plan-led development. As such, it is neither (r)evolutionary nor conventional. The challenge to contemporary practice that it poses does not require a paradigm shift, but it does require a significant change in tack. Herein lies a challenge for all urbanists to resolve, whatever their academic or professional background, and wherever their academic or professional allegiances lies.

2.2   TERMINOLOGY

2.2.1   The plot

The plot is an increment of landholding, set out for the express purpose of building.

Plots are usually described in two dimensions as a polygonal shape by metes and bounds, where the location of the vertices (the metes) of the plot are grid-referenced, and the length and direction of the line segments joining the metes (the bounds) are described in terms of their length and direction.

In US terminology, the equivalent noun is plat. According to *The Dictionary of Urbanism* the word plat originates from a combination of Old English plot (a piece of land) and Middle English plat (something flat). The process of setting out a plan for plots is thus referred to as 'platting', where plots and supporting infrastructure – streets and open spaces – are mapped out in relation to each other, and the boundaries of each precisely defined. The resulting map is sometimes referred to as a cadastre or a cadastral map, derived from the Greek *kata stikhon*, meaning 'line by line'.[26]

Dividing land into two or more plots is referred to as subdivision, and its opposite, the joining together of plots, is referred to as amalgamation, or sometimes consolidation. Parcels of land in general, and urban blocks in particular – the land defined by streets and public spaces – can be more or less subdivided into plots, or can comprise a single plot.

In some common law jurisdictions such as England, Wales and Ireland, the process of subdivision is a legal one, carried out through conveyance, where the resulting plot is described and recorded in a land registry, but not in any coordinated fashion in relation to those around it. The pattern of land subdivision in the UK and Ireland is effectively a product of the diverse and often competing interests of private individuals, developers and their agents that is shaped and reshaped in an ad hoc manner over time.

This contrasts with some other jurisdictions, notably the United States and Australia, where the regulation of subdivision provides the planning authority with a powerful additional means of controlling urban form. Regulation of subdivision by a central authority also facilitates the compilation of an urban cadastral map and, more importantly, allows the implications of subdivision on built form and on the overall pattern of subdivision to be considered.

Plots can take any shape; however, rectangular plots with the short side of the rectangle fronting the street are the most common. The extent of the plot that is directly accessible from the street is its frontage. A 'flagpole' plot is one without full frontage, necessitating access either by a narrow strip or by rights of way over another plot that connects it to the street. Plots may be laid out back to back, backing onto a secondary access street or lane (e.g. a mews), or they may have frontage to both sides of an urban block.

Although a plot may or may not be occupied by a building, one of its defining characteristics for the purposes of this book is that it is set out with the intention of being so occupied, in contrast to, say, a vegetable plot, which is laid out for the sole purposes of growing food. The relevance of this distinction is that although plots vary greatly in their size and shape, there is, in practice, a lower limit to the size and shape capable of accommodating any given building type.

The plot's legal status as a measured piece of land confers an independence from other landholdings that holds the key to its potential to be different from its neighbours, allowing diversity to be generated at different scales and intensities depending on the size and concentration of plots in relation to each other.

Academic research highlighting the importance of the plot as a determinant of urban form was pioneered by studies of plot patterns in historic towns, notably those conducted by Conzen in the 1960s. Conzen showed how the form of towns (which he referred to as 'townscape') was determined by three elements: the pattern of streets and plots (which he referred to as the 'town plan'); the building fabric; and the pattern of building and land uses.[27] For Conzen, the pattern of streets and plots is the most important of these because it frames the other two. He goes on to argue that the individual plot is the most appropriate spatial scale at which to ground such studies 'because it represents the smallest expression of undivided ownership, and therefore decision making, within the townscape'.[28]

2.2.2 The parcel

This term is increasingly used in the context of larger land-holdings in single ownership, often, for example, by volume house builders. Use of this term implies a distinction between parcels and plots, which are identified by the *Urban Design Compendium* as forming the basis for much of our built heritage. The *Compendium* notes that in masterplanning large areas there may be an opportunity to subdivide parcels into smaller parcels and/or plots to enable a range of developers to participate, thereby generating a richer mix of building types, tenures and uses.[29] Similarly, *Preparing Design Codes: A Practice Manual*[30] defines the parcel as a sub-area or phase of a larger site divided and sold off for development.

2.2.3 The block

The block is described by the *Urban Design Compendium* as the land area defined by the grid of streets: 'It can vary considerably in shape and size according to the configuration of streets, preferred orientation and topography, for instance, as well as the nature of plot subdivisions and building types that are to be accommodated.'[31]

Understanding the value of close-grain plots occupied by street buildings or townhouses requires an appreciation of alternative building typologies. The three most basic types are the perimeter block, the terrace and the pavilion block (or 'solitaire'), each of which carries different implications in terms of the grain of plot subdivision, built form and urban quality.

The perimeter block

The perimeter block typology has been a staple of urban development from ancient times, with many examples provided by 6th and 5th century BC Greek colonies. Roman town planning also adopted the perimeter block typology, and both favoured a regular orthogonal grid pattern. The perimeter block survived and mutated into a seemingly more organic form during the medieval period and saw a renaissance in the neo-classical era, before falling out of favour in the early 20th century.

The defining characteristic of the perimeter block identified by the *Urban Design Compendium* is that the edges of the block are lined with buildings. According to the *Compendium*, this is the best way to accommodate a diversity of building types and uses at medium to high densities, while ensuring that building frontages relate positively to the public realm.[32]

Perimeter blocks can be broken down into close-, medium- and coarse-grain plots, or they may be constructed on a single plot. Like the terrace, the massing of medium- or coarse-grain perimeter blocks is oriented to the street and so defines space in a similar way. The interior of the block may be left open as private or shared open space.

The rational form of blocks can provide for economical densities and can be adapted to different shapes. The rear of the block is flexible, allowing different uses to be incorporated. During the medieval period, it was common for commercial and industrial activities to take place in the interior of the block. Nuisance associated with these activities led to a

Principal block typologies.

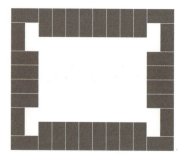
△ Perimeter block (close grain)

△ Perimeter block (medium grain)

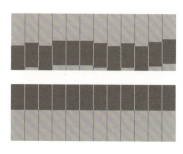
△ Terrace (close grain)

△ Open row (close grain)

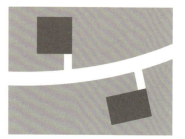
△ Pavilion block (coarse grain)

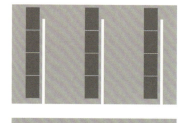
△ Pavilion block (medium grain)

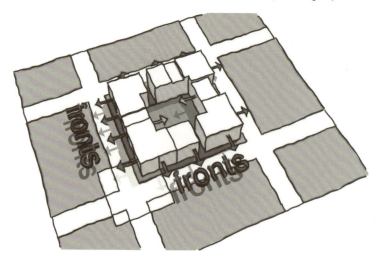

▷ The perimeter block typology clearly distinguishes between 'fronts' and 'backs'

move away from mixed-use blocks in the 20th century, and now most blocks are designed for single use, as either apartments or offices.[33]

A variant of the medium- to coarse-grain perimeter block is the courtyard block, where the main focus of internal spaces is to the inside of the block rather than to the street. This type of block is usually accessed from within the block, resulting in a less clear distinction between the front and the back. Historical examples of this type include courtyard houses, monastic cloisters, colleges and farmyard clusters.

The terrace

Small plots occupied by continuous terraces of street buildings (or townhouses) are perhaps the oldest and most versatile of urban building typologies. The terrace joins together individual plots in straight, curved or cranked lines. Because they derive their overall form from being joined together, they create an urban context that is greater than the sum of its parts. Terraces can be extended indefinitely; however, capacity of infrastructure, walkability and the need to access land behind the terrace effectively limits its length.

To avoid the problems associated with linear development (often referred to as 'ribbon development'), the terrace can be turned or 'cranked' to form more economical units in the form of perimeter blocks, fill gaps or join other blocks. In this way, terraces can be combined to form part of a cohesive spatial web.

A variant of this form is the open row, where buildings have gaps between them: for example, detached or semi-detached houses. Terraces and open rows, being composed of individual plots joined together, have an inherent flexibility and capacity for diversity, but the capacity for open rows to enclose urban space is diluted, particularly where the building line is set back from the street.

Terraces and open rows are adaptable to changes in topography. They can be one-sided or two-sided. They can be composed of buildings with different heights, widths, layout, function and appearance, or they can adopt identical designs with single functions. In the case of row housing, designs are usually replicated to obtain economies of scale, which also reduces diversity.

The terrace clearly defines space and distinguishes between its front and back. The façade of the terrace usually follows a more or less continuous building line, often up to the front of its plot. Backs are usually less formal, with greater variation, reflecting individual needs and preferences.

The pavilion block

The pavilion block (sometimes called the 'solitaire') is a type of freestanding building on an individual plot. Historically, these are building types that separated themselves from the network of urban elements made up of terraces or perimeter blocks, or stood separately in the landscape: for example, churches or castles. In urban contexts they were typically buildings with civic functions that were larger in scale than the general 'fabric' of the city they served.

Pavilion blocks can take the form of towers, slabs, cubes or other shapes, thus allowing great freedom of architectural expression. Their freestanding nature provides pavilion blocks with the flexibility to adapt to changing topography; however, they do not always have a direct relationship with the buildings or spaces around them.

In exposed locations, where pavilion blocks do not define the space around them, the resultant ambiguity between fronts and backs can be problematic. In an urban context, such blocks can be integrated into surrounding buildings to form one side of a space. In the case of higher buildings, one may overshadow another, and there may be undesirable microclimatic effects on balconies and at ground level.

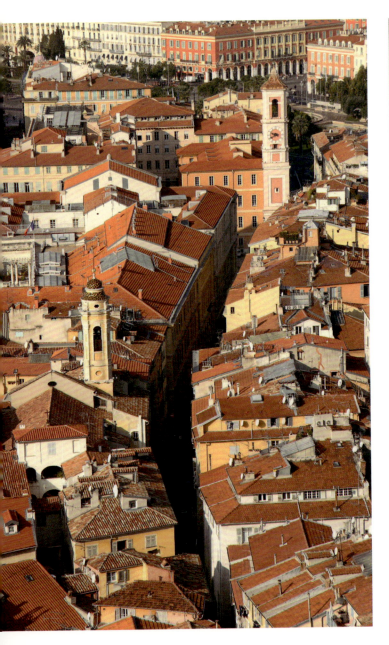

The Modern Movement in architecture promoted a changed concept of urban (and suburban) space which favoured freestanding buildings oriented towards the sun and placed freely in a man-made landscape, with the intention that space would be allowed to flow freely around (and under) the buildings. In other words, it was more concerned with the buildings than with the spaces between them.

While the buildings themselves often came to be treated as semi-sculptural objects, their physical and functional separation from the street eroded the street's ability to perform its traditional function as both a 'link' and a 'place'. It thus lost its multipurpose role as a corridor for different modes of movement and access and as a backdrop for street life and activity.

Oscar Newman pioneered research into the differences in crime rates between high-rise apartment buildings and low-rise buildings in New York, and his influential book on the subject, published in 1972, introduced the concept of 'defensible space' to explain them. This concept, in essence,

△ A modern close-grain street of townhouses, Steigereiland, Ijburg, the Netherlands

◁ Interior of a modern close-grain perimeter block, Tübingen, Germany

◁◁ A traditional close-grain street punctuated by a pavilion block in the form of a church

postulated that territoriality and surveillance of shared space has the potential to influence social behaviours for better or worse.

Freestanding towers and slab blocks did not contribute to a sense of enclosure or ownership of the territory around them. This space was neither wholly private nor wholly public, so responsibility for it was ambiguous. Combined with issues of location and tenure, the social consequences of deprivation and the inability of residents to maintain large areas of undefined space themselves meant that the spaces around them tended to become neglected, bleak and frequently hostile.

A commercial variant of the pavilion is the 'super shed'. These are also freestanding units, which, to the extent they do not attempt to establish any spatial or contextual reference, can be characterised as anti-urban. Sheds are usually large-span, freestanding structures, situated in large surface car parks, that are designed to accommodate retail warehousing or similar functions.

2.2.4 Urban grain

The 'grain' of urban development is a descriptive term that uses wood as a metaphor for the density and pattern of subdivision of blocks and plots. Close-, or 'fine-' grain places have a relatively dense pattern of subdivision, compared with medium- or 'coarse-' grain ones. Close-grain patterns may be occupied by detached, semi-detached or terraced rows, and by mixed-use or single-use buildings. They may be characterised by having buildings with no set-back from the street, or by uniform or varied set-backs. Similarly, they may be occupied by buildings that are varied in size and appearance, or identical.

Close-grain plot subdivisions often coincide with more or less continuous terraces of mixed-use street buildings that define and provide a sense of enclosure to the street. Streets defined in this way may be predominantly linear or they may comprise a grid of urban blocks. In some contexts, 'urban grain' is also used to refer to the size of urban blocks: the smaller the block, the greater the number of blocks and streets over a given urban area, providing a more permeable urban structure overall.

Medium- or coarse-grain urban blocks can define and enclose streets in the same way as close-grain ones, but they are made up of fewer property subdivisions. As a result, they tend to comprise fewer buildings, with less variety in appearance and fewer entrances to the street.

2.2.5 Density

Density in an urban design and planning context refers to the number of people in a given area. Higher densities are generally considered to be more sustainable than lower densities, because they make more efficient use of land, infrastructure and services and reduce dependence on car transport. At the urban level, the most widely applicable measure of density is expressed as residential dwelling units per hectare (dph). This is the most quoted measure and the most useful one for estimating development land requirements, making housing land allocations, monitoring completions/take-up and providing a broad indication of the intensity of development envisaged on a site or area.[34]

Estimates of need or viability of services and facilities, however, are based on the density of population, typically expressed as persons per hectare (ppha), rather than on residential dwelling units per hectare (dph). This is because it is the number of people concentrated in a given area that determines the viability of any given service, not the number of dwellings *per se*. In addition, the measure of dwellings per hectare masks the effect of the size of dwellings on population and, in turn, differences in the occupancy rates of dwellings. This can be misleading, for example, in an area dominated by large apartments (e.g. mansion blocks) as opposed to studio apartments.

Unless otherwise stated, most references to density assume *net* residential density. Net residential density only includes those areas used for housing and directly associated uses within the site, such as incidental open space, parking, play and internal access roads. The calculation of gross density includes areas not directly related to the site – typically roads and transport infrastructure, open space *and* other land uses.

Caution is also warranted because the relationship between net and gross densities is not directly proportional. While increasing *net residential densities* reduces the amount of *residential land* needed, above about 70 units per hectare the potential savings diminish as density rises and there is no effect on the amount of land needed for other uses.[35] Therefore, at the neighbourhood or district level, density standards need to make an allowance for the amount of land required for other uses.

But while net densities for notional single-use developments are relatively easy to estimate, more 'realistic' (i.e. gross density) figures can only be approximated because the influence of uses such as open space vary locally and can only be

△△ Close- (or 'fine-') grain (mixed-use) plot subdivision, Waterford

△◁ Coarse-grain (mixed-use) plot subdivision, Dublin

◁ Close-grain (single-use) subdivision, Dublin

calculated on a case-by-case basis 'on the ground'. According to the Department of the Environment, Heritage and Local Government (DEHLG) *Guidelines for Planning Authorities on Sustainable Residential Development in Urban Areas*, the area of land needed for such uses may be upwards of 25% of the net area.[36] Similarly, standards for open space vary and there is an increasing move away from quantitative standards for public open space towards qualitative ones, focused on design quality over quantity.

Average household size can be applied to measures of either net or gross units per hectare to estimate gross and net persons per hectare (ppha) respectively. The most commonly applied assumption of average household size for calculation purposes is 2.4 persons per dwelling (2.36 in 2001, down from 2.51 in 1991, according to census figures for England and Wales). Where residential uses are supplemented by significant employment uses, however, the transient population that is present during the working week may also need to be calculated in order to check the viability of some uses.

2.2.6 Diversity

Diversity is listed in *By Design* as one of seven mutually reinforcing characteristics of successful places.[37] Places characterised by diversity are defined in *By Design* as having variety and choice, including a mix of compatible developments and uses that work together to create viable places that respond to local needs.

Creating places that respond to local needs is not a new concern. The influential Tudor Walters Report on housing for the working classes, published in 1918, summarises the issue as follows:

> It is not enough merely to cover the ground with streets and houses. The site should be considered as the future location of a community mostly engaged in industrial pursuits having many needs

in addition to that of house room. Their social, educational, recreational and other requirements should, therefore, be considered and, when not already adequately provided for on the surrounding areas, should be met as part of the layout of the scheme. [38]

The report goes on to argue that provision of such facilities and services will enhance the attraction and value of the dwellings and, in relation to variety and social mixing (despite being primarily concerned with the 'economy and dispatch' of providing dwellings for the working classes), states:

> It is generally agreed that to cover large areas with houses, all of one size, and likely to be occupied by one class of tenant, unrelieved by any other types of dwelling occupied by different classes of society, is most undesirable, even when the depressing effect of monotonous unbroken rows is avoided.

The significance of diversity in an urban design context was championed by Jane Jacobs in her influential book published in 1961, *The Death and Life of Great American Cities*.[39] For Jacobs, the first and foremost question about the planning of cities is 'how can they generate enough mixture among uses – enough diversity – throughout their territories, to sustain their own civilization?'[40] Although she doesn't quite qualify what she means by civilisation, she goes on to warn that the alternative to diversity – monotony – leads not just to inconvenience, a lack of commercial choices and cultural interest, but to danger. Jacobs concludes that four conditions are indispensable to the generation of 'exuberant diversity':

☐ the district must be multi-functional
☐ most blocks must be small
☐ there must be a mingling of close-grain buildings of different ages and value
☐ there must be a sufficiently dense concentration of people.

The *Urban Design Compendium* concurs that successful communities require a full range of local services and facilities, including commercial, health, spiritual and civic uses, and that, critically, these need to be conveniently sited and accessible to residential areas by safe and comfortable walking routes. Notwithstanding the *Compendium*'s implicit separation of residential use from other uses, this introduces the notion of distance, and, in turn, the concentration of uses together, that results in one place being more or less diverse than another. The physical spread of traditional town centres that developed before car transport was self-limited by the distance people could walk comfortably. This generated demand for plots close to the centre and, consequently, the density of plot subdivision: urban grain.

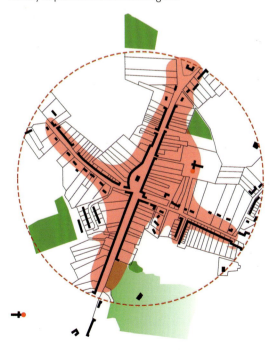

△ Traditional town centre with 400 m walkband (dashed line), Abbeyleix, County Laois, Ireland

In the context of the built environment, diversity encompasses a range of physical and intangible factors, each of which can be examined at different scales: the neighbourhood, urban form, urban space and built form.

The defining characteristic of diversity in an urban context is that it describes difference or heterogeneity, as opposed to its opposite: homogeneity. This means, of course, that diversity is not a simple 'yes/no', but can be observed to occur at different degrees of intensity and across different sectors: community, economy and place.

For the purposes of this book, diversity is expressed in terms of the following key indicators, subject to certain caveats:

☐ land uses – retail, office, residential, community services, live-work
☐ housing types – apartments, single family dwelling houses, duplex, maisonettes etc.
☐ house sizes – measured in terms of bedrooms or bed spaces
☐ tenure – private sector owned, private sector rental, rent controlled or affordable
☐ urban form – block type, building size and shape, massing
☐ urban grain – plot size and shape
☐ variety – design (and age) of buildings.

Land use categories such as 'shops', however, which are accorded their own 'Use Class Order' under planning legislation – meaning that permission is not generally required for change of use within a given use class, e.g. from one kind of shop to another, whereas permission is normally required to change between use classes – can mask important shades of difference.

Whether a shop or business is locally owned and operated as opposed to being owned and operated by a multiple retailer has been shown to have a significant effect on its potential to be different, as well as on its social and economic relations with surrounding businesses and customers.[41] Similarly, the definition of a shop, for example, does not distinguish between shops selling groceries (convenience goods), or clothes or shoes (comparison goods), or whether it is a pet shop or an undertaker's premises.

It is also worth considering that, particularly in terms of urban form, uniformity of appearance within a close-grain block subdivision is not always a bad thing. The uniformity of design and of materials of set piece blocks, for example, can be the characteristic that gives a unique identity.

Ultimately, it is the diversity of the human population – in terms of age, gender, ethnicity, education, occupation, socio-economic background – that contributes to the generation of diverse urban environments. Although it is not the role of urban design to create diverse populations, designers *are* required to ensure that places are universally accessible to people from every walk of life regardless of age, disability or any other characteristic.

2.2.7 Sustainability

Sustainability implies the capacity to endure. Cullingworth points out that the overwhelming political consensus on the importance of sustainability is an indicator of how widely it can be interpreted.[42] Cowan's *The Dictionary of Urbanism*, for example, refers to 13 different interrelated definitions, including the most commonly cited, which is set out in the World Commission on Environment and Development report *Our Common Future* (known as the Brundtland Report), published in 1987. According to the report, sustainable development 'meets the needs of the present without compromising the ability of future generations to meet their own needs'.[43]

The scope of sustainable urban design is particularly broad because it includes not only the capability of the natural environment to endure, but also that of the built environment: the place, its community *and* its economy. This parallel concern with sustaining nature and the economy at the same

△ This set piece Regency façade in Hove
masks the subdivision of the block into
separate residential plots

time is a source of tension when it comes to interpreting what sustainability means in practice.

The EU Ministerial note on sustainability published in 2006, known as the Bristol Accord, conflates the definitions of sustainable communities and sustainable places, stating that 'sustainable communities are places where people want to live and work, now and in the future. They meet the diverse needs of existing and future residents, are sensitive to their environment, and contribute to a high quality of life. They are safe and inclusive, well planned, built and run, offer equality of opportunity and good services for all.'[44] Although 'community' is not defined in this context, it implies some geographically defined settlement as opposed to, say, the 'academic community' or such like. More significantly, it explicitly refers to the mixing of primary activities, namely living and working, as well as secondary activities, such as the services required to meet the needs of existing and future residents.

More recently, the government has sought to add weight to economic criteria by introducing a 'presumption in favour of sustainable development'. As outlined in the National Planning Policy Framework (NPPF), it believes the purpose of the planning system is to contribute to sustainable development. The policies set out in the NPPF (taken as a whole) now constitute the government's view of what sustainable development means. In this context, it sees the planning system as performing three interrelated roles:

☐ an economic role: contributing to building a strong, responsive and competitive economy, by ensuring that sufficient land of the right type is available in the right places and at the right time to support growth and innovation; and by identifying and coordinating development requirements, including the provision of infrastructure

☐ a social role: supporting strong, vibrant and healthy communities, by providing the supply of housing required to meet the needs of present and future generations; and by creating a high-quality built environment, with accessible local services that reflect the community's needs and support its health, social and cultural well-being

☐ an environmental role: contributing to protecting and enhancing our natural, built and historic environment; and, as part of this, helping to improve biodiversity, use natural resources prudently, minimise waste and pollution, and mitigate and adapt to climate change, including moving to a low-carbon economy.[45]

Drawing on the work of the Department for Environment, Food and Rural Affairs (DEFRA), which tries to draw out the components of sustainable communities in more detail, it is suggested that sustainable communities are vibrant, with thriving local economies, a strong sense of identity and respect for their built and natural environment.[46]

Vibrant communities are:

☐ inclusive and fair
☐ healthy and safe
☐ aware and involved.

Thriving local economies are:

☐ vital
☐ diverse
☐ integrated
☐ well branded.

Places with a healthy environment and a sense of identity are:

☐ characterful
☐ attractive
☐ environmentally sensitive
☐ well connected.

Sustainable communities are places with...

A vibrant local community that is:

Community **1**	Inclusive and fair	Healthy	Aware & involved	Has a strong identity
	Tolerant and cohesive	A range of public, private, community and voluntary services that are appropriate to people's needs	Effective and inclusive participation representation and leadership	A strong sense of identity and civic pride
	Accessible to all			
	Fair to everyone, including those in other communities	Opportunities for sports and leisure, walking and cycling		
	Considerate of future generations	Safe, with low levels of crime and anti-social behaviour		

A thriving local economy that is:

**Economy** **2**	Vital	Diverse	Integrated	Well branded
	A flourishing and diverse local economy	A close grain of compatible land uses	Good services and communications	Marketing
	An economically viable centre	Variety and choice	Strong links to the rural hinterland, the region and the national economy	
	Local job opportunities	Appropriate and adaptive re-use of buildings		

A healthy environment and a strong sense of identity that is:

Place **3**	Characterful	Attractive	Environmentally sensitive	Well connected
	A strong sense of place, local identity and character	Featuring a high quality built and natural environment	Considerate to the environment	Good public transport connections, linking people to jobs, schools and health services
		Activated and well used public realm	Minimises climate change	Well managed traffic with an appropriate level of parking
		Appropriateness of size, scale, density, design and layout that complements local character	Makes efficient use of resources	Green infrastructure
		A tidy and clean public realm	Enhances biodiversity	
		Well maintained building fabric, respectful of the place's heritage character	Sources food locally	

△ The goal of sustainable communities

The Department for Communities and Local Government's (DCLG) *Preparing Design Codes: A Practice Manual* takes this further by identifying eight objectives for sustainable urban design: resource efficiency, diversity and choice, human needs, resilience, pollution reduction, concentration, distinctiveness and biotic support. Some of these (e.g. diversity and choice) overlap with broader urban design objectives, and are particularly relevant to urban grain.

Under the heading of diversity and choice, for example, the DCLG manual advocates mixed uses along streets and within buildings, mixed building types, ages and tenures, and mixed house sizes and specifications. The heading of human needs also encompasses a range of relevant sub-objectives, including design to human scale, visually interesting buildings, active frontages and entrances to the street, and natural surveillance. The heading of resilience includes designing

for 'fine-grain changes of use' and design for revitalisation of existing areas and heritage assets. In a similar vein, concentration implies building at densities that can sustain a viable range of uses and facilities, and vitality through concentration and compact building forms such as terraces. A more detailed account of the relationship between density and population catchments for uses and facilities is provided in Chapter 5.

2.3   THE PLOT SO FAR

The laying out of streets and plots is a fundamental act of place-making. Once a grid of streets is laid out, a second, more detailed grid of plots is put in place that is neither planned nor wholly unplanned, determined by the premeditated and spontaneous decisions of individuals over time, whose private interests transform the block: 'The dialectical relationship between street and built plots creates the tissue and it is in the continuation of this relationship – capable of modification, extension and the substitution of buildings – where reside the capacity of the city to adapt to the demographic, economic and cultural changes that mark its evolution.'[47]

The city is never static and, with a few exceptions to prove the rule, is constantly reshaped within its pre-existing frame of streets, and manifested through changes of plot configuration and the building structures that occupy it.

Close-grain plots are a legacy of traditional street patterns that define our most pleasing streets and places. They are a feature of places with lively and vibrant street life, variety, adaptability and richness of the public domain.

During the medieval period, burgage – an ancient land term meaning a town rental property owned by the king or lord – plots of varying widths and sizes were commonly granted in return for services, produce or money (tenure). Where these plots were not based on pre-existing (e.g. Roman) grid patterns, they tended to follow more irregular street patterns and topography. These plots were occupied by millers and

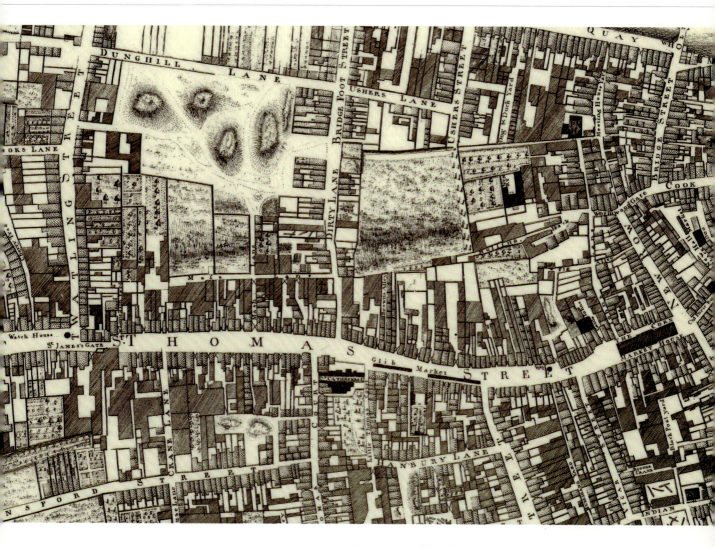

◁ Georgian town houses, Merrion Square,
Dublin

△ Extract from Roque's 1756 survey
of Dublin

bakers, tanners, felt makers, weavers, potters and black-
smiths, and their like, and gradually subdivided and built up to
enclose new streets. The street building (burgage tenement)
emerged as the staple building block of the medieval street.
Saving space, the plot was usually developed up to its front
boundary, providing a direct interface with the street. The rear
overlooked private gardens and courtyards that could be used
to absorb more building if additional space was needed.

Medieval plots were commonly measured in perches (poles
or rods), measuring 16½ feet (5.5 yards or 5 metres) in
length. This method was carried forward from the Roman
era, and equated to the amount of land a farm labourer was
expected to be able to work in one day: 1 acre = 1 furlong [a
long furrow] x 4 perches [1 chain].[48] Likewise, building construction was largely undertaken by hand, effectively limiting
its scale to human proportions.

Though typologically similar, these buildings were used for many different purposes and were expressed differently – depending on the needs and resources of the owner – and scaled according to centuries-old traditions of building by hand.

During the 18th century, estate owners began to lay out new streets and plots beyond the medieval core and to grant leases for their development according to stricter rules. These reverted to classical ideas of order and harmony, and manifested themselves once more in regular grids. Victorian developers began, incrementally, to join plots for purpose-built commercial premises, such as banks. What they shared with the medieval period, however, was the street as the vital structuring element of the city, and a fine grain of small plots developed individually or in small groups.

This mode of development began to fall out of favour with the advent of 20th-century land use planning. High population densities led to overdevelopment of burgage plots and, combined with poor sanitation, generated slum conditions that discredited the traditional urban block and street buildings as a typology.

The late 19th/early 20th-century Garden City Movement sought to marry the advantages of city and country life in a kind of ru-urban idyll. The Garden City Movement was founded by Ebenezer Howard, who published his influential book *Tomorrow: A Peaceful Path to Real Reform* in 1898 (reissued as *Garden Cities of Tomorrow* in 1902).

Howard's ideas found form initially in two garden cities – Letchworth Garden City and Welwyn Garden City – but they were even more influential in new suburban developments, such as Hampstead Garden Suburb. New suburbs were set out at lower densities with open rows of semi-detached houses on larger plots, set back from the access road and provided with long back gardens to encourage home-based agriculture. Raymond Unwin, the chief architect (with Barry Parker) of Letchworth and Hampstead, also

contributed to the influential Tudor Walters Report on housing for the working classes in 1918, which contained detailed recommendations on density and space standards that encouraged larger suburban plots. These standards were institutionalised by the Housing Manual and Housing Act of 1919, and were particularly influential on council housing. The Housing Manual was revised in 1944 and continued to influence suburban development thereafter.

A long-standing legacy of Unwin's recommendations, for example, is the commonplace local authority requirement for a separation distance of at least 21 m (70 feet) between facing windows,[49] which has exerted significant influence on plot depth ever since, particularly for suburban housing. In any case, Howard's more lofty ideals were frequently lost on mass house builders in the private sector, who were to become more concerned with how Ford-ist principles of mass production could be applied over swathes of identical plots to meet the demand of a new middle class of homeowner.

2.4 HOW WE LOST THE PLOT

A wide variety of macro-processes have driven changes in urban morphology with consequences for the integrity of traditional urban forms impacting on the plot. The relative influence of these has varied from place to place and over time, necessitating a degree of generalisation to highlight some general trends.

There is a historical tendency for larger parcels to be subdivided into smaller ones as the supply of land decreases and demand for it increases, generating a fascinating and character-full patchwork of form in older cities, towns and villages, that is neither wholly planned, nor wholly unplanned.[50] This rich tapestry, however, has been unravelled through a variety of macro-processes such as commercial property speculation, the so-called 'retail revolution', traffic and road widening. Left to decay and eventual collapse, street buildings are lost and increasingly are

Losing the plot in Smithfield, Dublin, 1756–2010.

△ 1756: Plots 73; Buildings 71

△ 1847: Plots 65; Buildings 61

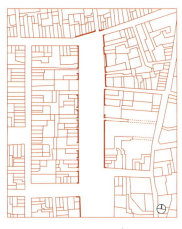

△ 1936: Plots 57; Buildings 48

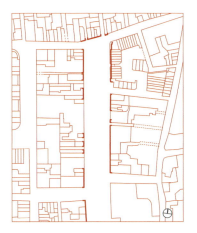

△ 1983: Plots 53; Buildings 44

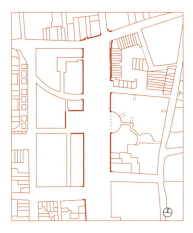

△ 2010: Plots 30; Buildings 29

followed by amalgamation of their plots into larger parcels, producing the opposite of diversity: a monoculture of land uses, monolithic building forms and segregated communities.

Following the widespread destruction of urban areas during World War II, new ideas for the construction of planned and rational cities based on a separation of their four main functions – living, working, recreation and transport – were widely adopted in plans for reconstruction and rehousing worldwide. These ideas were promulgated by the Athens Charter that emerged from the Congrès International d'Architecture Moderne (CIAM) held in 1933 (published a decade later by Le Corbusier); however, the results were often inflexible and inhumane, and in any case were more concerned with the design of buildings than with the spaces between them.

This preoccupation with zoning land for single uses, along with slum clearance, growth of car ownership and the emergence of a more speculative commercial development market, led ultimately to a process of suburbanisation, and latterly 'de-urbanisation'. This was paralleled in many urban areas by urban decay, obsolescence and the amalgamation of smaller urban plots into larger redevelopment sites. Meanwhile, a suburban-based factory system of production progressively replaced the pre-existing urban-centred workshop system and, combined with retail concentration, further undermined the commercial stability of the urban street.

As a result, the laying out of compact networks of streets and mixed-use plots in the city was supplanted in the suburbs by a preference for freestanding buildings surrounded by car-parking and by mass-produced low-rise (and lower-cost) housing accessed via highly engineered, yet poorly connected, distributor roads.

Within towns and cities the equilibrium between 'link' and 'place' functions of mixed-use streets was disturbed by policies that prioritised the speed and efficiency of vehicular traffic movement over pedestrian movement. This generated a hostile environment and further undermined the viability of the street as a 'place' in its own right.

One more stake in the heart of the traditional mixed-use street was driven by the innovation of the shopping mall in the latter half of the 20th century. This conjoined two earlier innovations: the shopping arcade and the department store. The arcade, essentially a privately owned internal 'street', provided a new shopping environment protected from the grime and noise of the street, while the department store removed the barrier between the shopper and the goods, opening up the prospect of 'browsing' without any predetermined outcome. The classic 'dumb-bell' mall configuration thus provided a department store at each end of an arcade, acting as magnets to draw shoppers between the intervening retail units. This generated sufficient retail footfall in a pleasant environment, but located in the suburbs and accessed by car.

But the key factors that undermined the primacy of the urban block as the staple unit of urban form in the 19th and 20th centuries have eased. Population densities in cities have dropped radically since their height, while poor sanitation and pollution are no longer significant push factors. On the other hand, the coincidence of lower urban densities with smaller household sizes and better standards of living means neighbours have less need to rely on each other for mutual support, and there is less demand for street space

◁ Coarse-grain slab block in north Dublin

△ Illustrative proposal showing potential
for existing coarse-grain block to be
replaced with mixed-use, close-grain
street buildings

to be shared. Consequently, the use of residential streets for children's play, and as 'spill-out' space for families, is no longer a feature of towns and cities.

In relative terms, the suburban house that was affordable to the post-war generation on a single income now requires two incomes, and social problems are increasingly being associated with the suburbs rather than the city. The daily grind of commuting is no longer acceptable to many, and the paucity of community infrastructure, local services and recreational outlets available in the suburbs has contributed to something of an urban renaissance. There has been a resurgence in apartment living among a younger generation of people who now find it prohibitively expensive to finance their own property but still regard apartment living as a life stage on the path to ownership of a single family home in the suburbs.

The ad hoc development of close-grain mixed-use plots in older urban centres now survives (to a greater or lesser extent) as a legacy of an older system of development, which stands in stark contrast to the wholesale development of single-use plots in the suburbs. Meanwhile, the practice and potential for laying out plots in more sustainable patterns as a means of achieving diversity and choice both in existing urban centres and the suburbs seems to have been overlooked.

△ A typical shopping mall, showing how the function of the street is internalised

◁ In contrast to the privately owned shopping mall, traditional mixed-use street buildings are accessed from the public realm providing a backdrop for street life to take place

▷ A traditional mixed-use street

3 Guiding the plot

3.1 THE STATUS OF GUIDANCE

The current UK government believes that too much policy and guidance has been produced in the past, and that this has taken on a force that has constrained practitioners and users on the ground.[51] The policy and guidance that the government is referring to in this context are Planning Policy Statements (PPSs) and Planning Policy Guidance (PPGs), which have recently been replaced in England by a single, simplified statement of planning policy: the National Planning Policy Framework (NPPF).

Meanwhile, the devolved governments of Scotland, Wales and Northern Ireland will retain their existing planning policy documents, supported by Planning Advice Notes (PANs), Technical Advice Notes (TANs) and Supplementary Planning Guidance (SPGs) respectively. Planning policy in the Republic of Ireland is articulated separately through ministerial guidelines and related documents.

Underlying all of these layers, however, there exists a separate category of non-statutory guidance that can most usefully be described as 'best practice' urban design guidance.

Best practice urban design guidelines are not in themselves policy statements, nor are they policy guidance, but they have been developed in a policy context or as companions to policy. Policies are generated by the prevailing political regime and, as such, can and do change with successive administrations. However, the principles of 'good urban design' that are extrapolated in best practice guidelines and the underlying policy commitment to building more sustainable communities have not changed. Such guidelines can be read as an interpretation of how policies can be achieved in practice. As such, they have become more influential in planning and urban design practice than the policies themselves. It is the prevailing UK government's intention, however, to reduce the amount of non-statutory guidance in future and to shorten existing guidance.

This chapter summarises the planning policy frameworks currently operating in England and Wales, Scotland, Northern Ireland and the Republic of Ireland, highlighting their commitment to achieving diversity in new development. This is followed by a brief summary of the relationship between diversity and the wider objectives of urban design, in so far as these objectives have become embedded in contemporary 'best practice' guidelines. A range of different urban design guidelines are examined in turn, and the extent to which each identifies and promotes diversity, whether in general terms or specifically in terms of mixing uses, urban form and tenure, is explained, highlighting instances where they explicitly link diversity with urban grain.

3.2 PLANNING POLICY

3.2.1 The National Planning Policy Framework

The National Planning Policy Framework sets out the objectives for the planning system in the context of the government's economic, social and environmental priorities for England, including a presumption in favour of sustainable development. The NPPF thus consolidates and integrates all the previous national planning policies set out in PPSs and PPGs into a single document.

The NPPF promotes diversity both directly and indirectly:

- ☐ It sets out core planning principles that include the promotion of mixed-use developments that create more vibrant places.

- ☐ It promotes the vitality of town centres by requiring local planning authorities to allocate a range of suitable sites to meet the scale and type of retail, leisure, commercial, office, tourism, cultural, community and residential uses they need.

☐ It recognises that residential development can play an important role in ensuring the vitality of centres and requires local planning authorities to set out policies to encourage residential development on appropriate sites.

☐ It encourages local planning authorities to plan positively for town centres in decline.

☐ It requires local planning authorities to prioritise development in town centres over edge of centre or out of town sites, and to consider the impact of larger out of town developments (greater than 2,500 sq m) on choice and trade in the town centre.

☐ It advocates a balance of land uses so that people can be encouraged to minimise journey lengths for employment, shopping, leisure, education and other activities.

☐ It promotes a mix of uses in larger-scale residential developments to provide opportunities for people to undertake day-to-day activities, including work on site.

☐ It suggests (where practical) primary schools and local shops should be located within walking distance of most properties.

☐ It urges local planning authorities to create sustainable, inclusive and mixed communities, with a mix of housing based on current and future demographic trends, market trends and the needs of different groups in the community including families with children, older people, people with disabilities, service families and people wishing to build their own homes

☐ It encourages local planning authorities to plan positively for the provision and use of shared space, community facilities (such as local shops, meeting places, sports venues, cultural buildings, public houses and places of worship) and other local services to enhance the sustainability of communities and residential environments.

☐ It discourages local planning authorities from imposing architectural styles, stifling innovation, originality or initiative through unsubstantiated requirements to conform to certain development forms or styles.

☐ It advocates the use of design codes that avoid being overly prescriptive or detailed.

The NPPF's planning objectives will be delivered through a trimmed-down planning framework comprising the NPPF itself, Local and Neighbourhood Plans, and the development management system. The NPPF suggests, however, that local people (and local government) can produce their own distinctive Local and Neighbourhood Plans reflecting their own particular needs and priorities within this framework, provided they align the strategic priorities identified in the Local Plan.

The NPPF highlights the implications of its presumption in favour of sustainable development for communities engaged in neighbourhood planning. Specifically (and subject to being consistent with the Local Plan) they are encouraged to identify opportunities to use Neighbourhood Development Orders to enable developments that are consistent with their Neighbourhood Plan to proceed.

The supporting legislation for the NPPF thus empowers Neighbourhood Forums to prepare Neighbourhood Plans and, by way of Neighbourhood Development Orders and Community Right to Build Orders, to determine development proposals without planning permission as well as to bring forward their own development proposals.

The policy drive towards localism is increasingly being aligned with the potential for plot-based development to meet a range of related policy concerns, such as increasing housing supply, diversification of the building industry, afford-ability, local employment and choice. The government has responded by requesting the production of an Action Plan for the promotion of plot-based self building and commu-nity-led group schemes. The Action Plan, prepared by the National Self Build Association (NaSBA) on behalf of the joint government/industry Self Build Working Group, advo-cates a stronger recognition for the sector in national policy and the building of an evidence base to support local plan-ning policies to increase the supply of plots, alongside other recommendations to level the playing field between self builders and established house builders.

This more generalist approach contrasts with the Dutch Fifth National Policy on Spatial Planning 2000/2020, for example, which takes a more proactive approach by stipulating that one third of all new homes should be individually commis-sioned. Under the policy, groups or individuals acquire land for themselves as self builders, and commission architects of their own choice.[52]

The replacement of PPSs and PPGs by the much higher level of policy statements contained in the NPPF has the potential to sow the seeds of confusion (at best) or conflict (at worst) as to what the policy should mean in practice. For this reason, practitioners will need to become more aware of best practice guidance to support their own proposals, and as a means of interpreting the NPPF.

3.2.2 Planning Policy Wales

Planning Policy Wales (PPW), updated in 2011, is supple-mented by 21 topic-based Technical Advice Notes (TANs). Procedural guidance is also given in Welsh Office/National Assembly for Wales/Welsh Assembly Government circulars. PPW promotes the role of the planning system in delivering sustainable development in Wales, which is enshrined as a responsibility under the Government of Wales Act 2006.

The policy makes special reference to the role of mixed-use development, comprising appropriate combinations of housing (including affordable housing), employment, retail-ing, education, leisure and recreation uses and open space, in promoting both the vitality of town, district, local and vil-lage centres and the regeneration of urban areas. It also recognises the design opportunities afforded by mixed-use development and the importance of design for the success of compact mixed-use developments, for example in helping to keep noise levels low.[53] The importance of good design is reiterated and given further weight in supporting Technical Advice Note 12: Design.[54]

The main purpose of the policy is to provide a framework for the preparation of development plans by planning authori-ties, which, inter alia, are urged to:

☐ **encourage a wide range and mix of uses in town centres and other appropriate places to add activity and choice of places in which to live**

☐ **integrate different uses in accessible locations to increase social inclusion, reduce the need to travel and make towns safer for people both day and night**

☐ **promote the role of mixed-use development in increasing the feasibility of delivering local renewable and low-carbon energy solutions such as district heating schemes.[55]**

3.2.3 Scottish Planning Policy

Scottish Planning Policy (SPP), updated in 2010, is similar in format to PPW. One noteworthy provision of the policy states, however, that when considering the format, design and scale of proposals, developers, owners and occupiers should take into account the setting of the centre. In particu-lar, 'This should include considering different built forms for the development, adjusting or subdividing large proposals to better fit with existing development, and making use of vacant and under-used land or premises.'[56]

Another interesting feature is provision of specific technical guidance on masterplanning, through Planning Advice Note 83. This recognises that Scotland has historically benefited from imaginative but robust masterplans, such as Edinburgh New Town. It suggests we can learn from these precedents, often created by designers or builders working with a degree of freedom within a framework of rules. It goes on to describe how these rules often governed matters such as layout, size of plots, building heights, the line of building frontages and building materials.[57]

Though recognising the failure of masterplanning to realise its potential in recent developments in Scotland (and also promoting design coding as a delivery mechanism), it stops short of discussing the potential role of urban grain and plots in masterplanning new development.

3.2.4 Planning policy in Northern Ireland

Planning policy in Northern Ireland also comprises a rolling programme of topic-based Planning Policy Statements (PPSs), supported by Supplementary Planning Guidance (SPGs), including Development Control Advice Notes and guidelines. Planning in Northern Ireland is currently administered centrally by the Planning Service, an agency within the Department of the Environment; however, this is due to change. The overarching planning policy is set out in PPS1: General Principles, which describes the Department's overall approach to planning across the range of topics.

The Department's approach to planning is set out under the headings of:

- [ ] sustainable development
- [ ] quality development
- [ ] design considerations
- [ ] mixed uses.

A particular aim of PPS1 (NI) is to seek to promote and retain mixed uses, particularly in town centres, in other areas highly accessible by means of transport other than the private car, and in areas of major new development. New mixed-use developments, it suggests, should be characterised by:

- [ ] compactness
- [ ] a mixture of uses and dwelling types
- [ ] a range of employment, leisure and community facilities
- [ ] appropriate infrastructure and services
- [ ] high standards of urban design
- [ ] access to public open space and green spaces
- [ ] ready access to public transport
- [ ] facilitation of walking and cycling.[58]

3.2.5 Planning policy in the Republic of Ireland

Planning policy in Ireland is articulated through a combination of legislation, the National Spatial Strategy, Ministerial Circulars and topic-based Guidelines for Planning Authorities issued by the Department of Environment, Community and Local Government (formerly Environment, Heritage and Local Government). While these are termed 'guidelines', planning authorities are required by the planning acts to have regard to them in the exercise of their functions. This confers on them a quasi-statutory status; however, the line between what is guidance and what is mandatory is sometimes unclear. Some of these ministerial guidelines, including Guidelines for Planning Authorities on Sustainable Residential Development in Urban Areas and Guidelines for Planning Authorities on the Preparation of Local Area Plans, for example, are also accompanied by 'best practice' guidelines or manuals.

The main thrust of the Guidelines for Planning Authorities on Sustainable Residential Development in Urban Areas is to promote quality through plan-led, sequential development. In particular, it seeks to promote high-quality developments at sustainable densities that, inter alia:

☐ provide a good range of community and support facilities where and when needed that are easily accessible

☐ are easy to access for all and easy to find one's way around

☐ promote the efficient use of land and of energy, and minimise greenhouse gas emissions

☐ provide a mix of land uses to minimise transport demand

☐ promote social integration and provide accommodation for a diverse range of household types and age groups.[59]

3.3 DIVERSITY AND THE OBJECTIVES OF URBAN DESIGN

The objectives of urban design and what they mean for aspects of urban form are reproduced here from *By Design: Urban design in the planning system* to illustrate the relationship between these characteristics and urban grain, and to reinforce the relevance of diversity to successful placemaking. They also explain several of the terms used in policy and guidelines as well as throughout this book.

Because the objectives of urban design are themselves abstract in nature, they are supplemented by certain aspects of development form, that articulate how these objectives transpose into physical form. These aspects of form include urban grain, mix of uses and the relationship of buildings and uses to the street.

3.4 URBAN DESIGN GUIDELINES

The importance of diversity to creating successful places, and what this means for urban grain, is touched upon in numerous 'best practice' urban design guidelines. Some of the most significant are:

☐ *By Design: Urban design in the planning system – towards better practice*. Department of the Environment, Transport and the Regions (DETR) and the Commission for Architecture and the Built Environment (CABE), 2000.

☐ *Urban Design Compendium*. English Partnerships and the Housing Corporation, 2000.

☐ *By Design: Better places to live – a companion guide to PPG3*. Commission for Architecture and the Built Environment (CABE) and the Office of the Deputy Prime Minister (ODPM), 2001.

☐ *Building for Life: Delivering great places to live*. Commission for Architecture and the Built Environment (CABE), 2008.

☐ *Preparing Design Codes: A practice manual*. Department for Communities and Local Government (DCLG), 2006.

☐ *Urban Design Manual: A best practice guide – a companion document to the Guidelines for Planning Authorities on Sustainable Residential Development in Urban Areas*. Department of the Environment, Heritage and Local Government (DEHLG), 2009.

3.4.1 By Design: Urban design in the planning system – towards better practice

These guidelines were published by the Department of the Environment, Transport and the Regions (DETR) and the Commission for Architecture and the Built Environment (CABE) in 2000 as a companion to the then government's policy for design in the planning system – Planning Policy Guidance Note 1 (PPG1) General Policy and Principles – with the stated aim of promoting better design through the planning system.

The main body of the guidelines is focused on the systematic elaboration of the objectives of urban design and their implications for urban form as 'prompts to thinking'.

The guidelines promote two main aspects of diversity:

☐ mixing of uses at a variety of scales, i.e. within a neighbourhood (groups of uses next to each other) or street (one use next to another), or within individual buildings (one use above another)

☐ diversity of layout, building form and tenure.

They note that 'subdividing large sites into smaller development plots, each with direct access to public roads or spaces, can help create diversity, especially if different approaches to design are adopted, using different architects', and that 'narrow plot frontages can allow small scale shopping and commercial activities to flourish and adapt to changing needs'.

3.4.2 Urban Design Compendium

The *Urban Design Compendium* was developed alongside the Department of the Environment, Transport and the Regions (DETR) publication *By Design: Urban design in the planning system* in the wake of the report of the Urban Task Force, *Towards an Urban Renaissance*. The *Compendium*

was published by English Partnerships and the Housing Corporation in 2000, with the stated aim of equipping project applicants, funding bodies and interested parties with guidance on achieving and assessing the quality of urban design in developing and restoring urban areas. Its sister volume, *Urban Design Compendium 2: Delivering quality places*, was published by English Partnerships in 2007, with greater focus on case studies and examples.

The *Compendium* sets out the principles of urban design and best practice approaches to a range of urban design and planning issues, and promotes the benefits of mixing uses as follows:

☐ more convenient access to facilities
☐ reducing travel to work congestion
☐ increasing opportunities for social interaction
☐ more socially diverse communities
☐ visual stimulation and delight of different buildings within close proximity
☐ a greater feeling of safety, with 'eyes on the street'
☐ greater energy efficiency and more efficient use of space and buildings
☐ more consumer choice of lifestyle, location and building type
☐ urban vitality and street life
☐ increased viability of urban facilities and support for small businesses.

The *Compendium* describes how conventional approaches to land use planning have militated against achieving the benefits of mixing uses and suggests this tendency can be reversed by promoting diversity of:

☐ development forms
☐ land use
☐ density
☐ tenure
☐ market segments.

QUALITIES OF SUCCESSFUL PLACES	OBJECTIVES OF URBAN DESIGN
Character A place with its own identity	To promote character in townscape and landscape by responding to and reinforcing locally distinctive patterns of development, landscape and culture.
Continuity and enclosure A place where public and private spaces are clearly distinguished	To promote the continuity of street frontages and the enclosure of space by development which clearly defines public and private areas.
Quality of the public realm A place with attractive and successful outdoor areas	To promote public spaces and routes that are attractive, safe, uncluttered and work effectively for all in society, including disabled and elderly people.
Ease of movement A place that is easy to get to and move through	To promote accessibility and local permeability by making places that connect with each other and are easy to move through, putting people before traffic and integrating land uses and transport.
Legibility A place that has a clear image and is easy to understand	To promote legibility through development that provides recognisable routes, intersections and landmarks to help people find their way around.
Adaptability A place that can change easily	To promote adaptability through development that can respond to changing social, technological and economic conditions.
Diversity A place with variety and choice	To promote diversity and choice through a mix of compatible developments and uses that work together to create viable places that respond to local needs.

△ The objectives of urban design and their implications for urban form as outlined by the Department of the Environment Transport and the Regions (DETR) in its 2000 publication *By Design: Urban design in the planning system – towards better practice*

ASPECTS OF DEVELOPMENT FORM	EXPLANATION
Layout: urban structure The framework of routes and spaces that connect locally and more widely, and the way developments, routes and open spaces relate to one other.	The layout provides the basic plan on which all other aspects of the form and uses of a development depend.
Layout: urban grain The pattern and arrangement of street blocks, plots and their buildings in a settlement.	The degree to which an area's pattern of blocks and plot subdivisions is respectively small and frequent (fine-grain), or large and infrequent (coarse-grain).
Landscape The character and appearance of land, including its shape, form, ecology, natural features, colours and elements, and the way these components combine.	This includes all open space, including its planting, boundaries and treatment.
Density and mix The amount of development on a given piece of land and the range of uses. Density influences the intensity of development, and in combination with the mix of uses can affect a place's vitality and viability.	The density of a development can be expressed in a number of ways. This could be in terms of plot ratio (particularly for commercial developments), number of dwellings, or the number of habitable rooms (residential development).
Scale: height Scale is the size of a building in relation to its surroundings, or the size of parts of a building or its details, particularly in relation to the size of a person. Height determines the impact of development on views, vistas and skylines.	Height can be expressed in terms of the number of floors; height of parapet or ridge; overall height; any of these in combination; a ratio of building height to street width; height relative to particular landmarks or background buildings; or strategic views.
Scale: massing The combined effect of the arrangement, volume and shape of a building or groups of buildings in relation to other buildings and spaces.	Massing is the three-dimensional expression of the amount of development on a given piece of land.
Appearance: details The craftsmanship, building techniques, decoration, styles and lighting of a building or structure.	This includes all building elements such as openings and bays; entrances and colonnades; balconies and roofscape; and the rhythm of the façade.
Appearance: materials The texture, colour, pattern and durability of materials, and how they are used.	The richness of a building lies in its use of materials which contribute to the attractiveness of its appearance and the character of the area.

It goes on to describe development parcels as tracts of land, usually under a single ownership, which are the basis for most new developments, especially those driven by volume house builders. It contrasts parcels with plots, which it points out are usually much smaller increments or landholdings that form the basis for much of our built heritage – giving established centres their variety and urban grain.

The *Compendium* explicitly promotes the subdivision of parcels into smaller plots to be apportioned to different developers, enabling a range of developers to generate a richer mix of building types, tenures and uses. It recommends making plots as small and narrow as practicable to encourage a diversity of forms, uses and tenures and to allow a rich variety of buildings to emerge.

The *Compendium* suggests that this will also:

☐ generate more active frontage
☐ encourage human-scale development and fine pedestrian grain
☐ enable higher densities to be achieved (compared with pavilion block types)
☐ provide a flexible basis for amalgamation if necessary and to enable future incremental growth to take place
☐ minimise costly and wasteful leftover space.

The *Compendium* notes that the creation of socially mixed communities with varied lifestyles requires a mix of building types and settings and states that this can be achieved by creating a fine grain of plots and avoiding grouping too many lower-density units together. Although the *Compendium* and *Urban Design Compendium 2* provide examples of masterplans and buildings that provide for mixed uses, they focus on buildings rather than plots, and as a result avoid explaining how diversity can be delivered through close-grain plot typologies.

3.4.3 By Design: Better places to live – a companion guide to PPG3

By Design: Better places to live was published by the OPDM and CABE in 2001 to support the implementation of PPG3 (Housing) by promoting housing design quality and the principles of urban design. PPG3 sought to address the legacy of poorly designed low-density suburban development by:

☐ reviewing conventional road design standards
☐ encouraging more efficient use of land and higher densities
☐ requiring better mixes of dwelling sizes, types and affordability
☐ requiring a commitment to good urban design.

The guidelines promote mixed communities because they can:

☐ lead to a better demand for community services
☐ provide opportunities for 'lifetime communities'
☐ make neighbourhoods more robust by avoiding large concentrations of housing of the same type
☐ enable community 'self help'
☐ assist community surveillance by avoiding the creation of dormitory suburbs.

The guidelines also point out that a mix of housing types and uses can contribute to the creation of more attractive places by enabling diversity of building forms and scales:

☐ Apartments can give scale to focal points and turn corners with continuous frontage.

☐ Townhouses can contribute to formal compositions and frame open spaces.

☐ Community buildings can give status to civic spaces and provide a focus for community activity.

Chapter 5 of the guidelines – Housing layout and urban form – promotes the advantages of the perimeter block structure (whether orthogonal or 'organic' in character) and gives some consideration to the arrangement of dwellings within the block structure in terms of, for example, their plan form, treatment of corners and orientation of windows. However, in avoiding the issue of plot subdivision, it implicitly assumes housing developments will be designed and constructed on a block-by-block rather than a plot-by-plot basis.

Following a concern about so-called 'garden grabbing' by developers, PPS3 was amended in 2010 to exclude private residential developments from the definition of previously developed land and deleting the minimum indicative density requirement of 30 dwellings per hectare. This change was intended to give greater discretion to planning authorities in regard to both dual occupancy (subdivision) and the amalgamation of plots to facilitate larger infill or back-land type developments. It was carried out following a study[60] prepared on behalf of the government that considered that well-designed garden land development may add significantly to the housing stock in ways that are sustainable and meet identified local housing needs. It can:

☐ reduce the need to extend development into the countryside

☐ create new homes without the need for increased infrastructure provision

☐ provide better utilisation of land in areas where people no longer demand large gardens owing to lifestyle changes

☐ provide small sites appropriate for local developers who employ local people.

The National Planning Policy Framework, however, which now supersedes the regime of Planning Policy Statements and Planning Policy Guidance notes, adopts a still more ambiguous approach, stating that local planning authorities should set out their own approach to housing density to reflect local circumstances.[61]

3.4.4 Building for Life: Delivering great places to live

Building for Life (BfL) is the national standard for well-designed homes and neighbourhoods published by the Commission for Architecture and the Built Environment (CABE) on behalf of the Building for Life Partnership (comprising CABE, the Home Builders Federation (HBF) and Design for Homes) in 2008. BfL was established in 2001 following the publication of PPG3 as an initiative to showcase good design. It draws on the objectives of urban design along with a range of other guidelines, studies and Planning Policy Statements to provide a set of 20 questions that should be addressed in the design of new schemes.

The significance of BfL for practice is that it applies to mixed-use as well as residential schemes and provides a framework for assessing the quality of proposals that strongly influences how smoothly they are likely to progress through the planning system and their potential to secure public funding.

In particular, BfL requires consideration of community services and facilities (including shops, pubs and cafés), a mixture of housing types and sizes that reflects the needs and aspirations of the community, and a mix of social and privately rented accommodation, shared ownership and freehold market segments.

The future of BfL is currently being reviewed. Meanwhile the Design Council/CABE is continuing to encourage its use, and the Homes and Communities Agency (HCA) has maintained its requirement for schemes to achieve a BfL score of 12 or more in order to secure HCA funding.[62]

3.4.5 Preparing Design Codes: A practice manual

This manual, prepared by the DCLG in conjunction with CABE in 2006, maps a range of sustainability objectives, including diversity and choice, and distinctiveness, against four spatial scales: the settlement pattern, urban form, urban space and built form. In relation to urban form the manual advocates:

- a mix of uses within neighbourhoods
- design of fine-grain street and space networks
- support for diversity in neighbourhood character
- localised facilities and services.

At the level of built form, it recommends mixing uses within buildings, mixing building types and tenures, accessibility and adaptability, different dwelling sizes and specifications.

The National Planning Policy Framework suggests that local planning authorities should consider using design codes where they could help deliver high-quality outcomes. However, it recommends that design policies should avoid unnecessary prescription or detail and should concentrate on guiding the overall scale, density, massing, height, landscape, layout and access of new development in relation to neighbouring buildings and the local area more generally.[63]

3.4.6 Urban Design Manual: A best practice guide – a companion document to the Guidelines for Planning Authorities on Sustainable Residential Development in Urban Areas

Like *By Design: Better places to live*, this manual, published by the Department of the Environment, Heritage and Local Government (DEHLG) in Ireland in 2009, is focused on residential design quality. It sets out 12 criteria for consideration that represent a distillation of Irish policy and the principles of urban design at the scale of the neighbourhood, site and home:

Neighbourhood:

- context
- connections
- inclusiveness
- variety.

Site:

- efficiency
- distinctiveness
- layout
- public realm.

Home:

- adaptability
- privacy and amenity
- parking
- detailed design.

The manual states that the most successful – and sustainable – communities contain a variety of things to do, see and enjoy. This means providing a mix of uses, facilities and amenities. It lists positive indicators of variety as follows:

- Activities generated by the development contribute to the quality of life in its locality.
- Uses that attract the most people are in the most accessible locations.
- Neighbouring uses and activities are compatible with each other.
- Housing types and tenure add to the choice available in the area.
- Opportunities have been taken to provide shops, facilities and services that complement those already available in the neighbourhood.

The manual cautions, however, that potential conflict between residential and other uses in integrated mixed-use developments caused by noise, smell nuisance, tenure or parking needs to be resolved at the planning stage through design and/or management measures. It does not describe what design or management measures this might entail, or the role of plot subdivision in achieving variety.

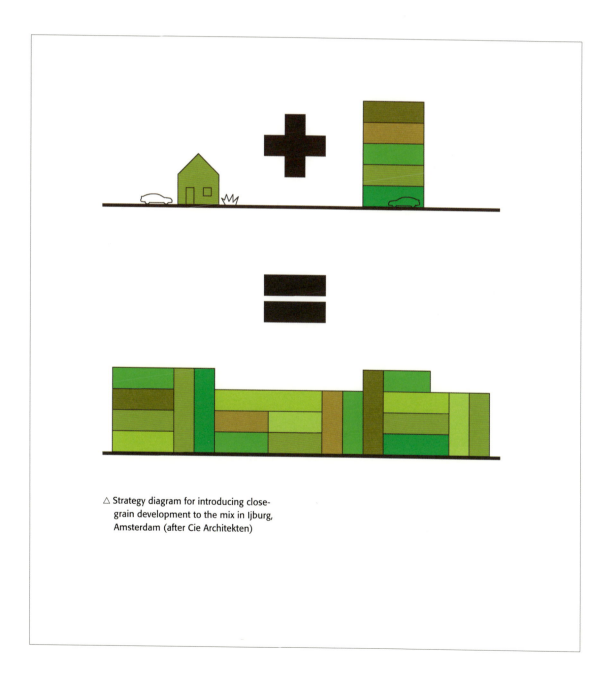

△ Strategy diagram for introducing close-
grain development to the mix in Ijburg,
Amsterdam (after Cie Architekten)

4 Developing the plot

Places that have succeeded in creating diversity have done so, by and large, by returning to traditional modes of development characterised by 'platting'. Critical infrastructure – streets and public spaces – has been forward-funded by the project proponents, to provide a range of serviced plots and/or blocks for sale to diverse interests, but within a pre-defined urban design framework or masterplan.

This isn't as straightforward as conventional modes of development, characterised by comprehensive development over a single landholding by a single developer. It requires leadership, coordination, a more integrated approach to design, phasing and forward funding of infrastructure, and a committed delivery vehicle.

Several factors contrive to help or hinder the prospects for developing close-grain plots in general, and mixed-use ones in particular. Alone and in concert, these have the potential either to perpetuate the status quo, or to unlock the potential for developing more sustainable places, characterised by variety and choice.

These factors range from property market preferences on the part of developers, investors and homebuyers, and financial constraints affecting forward funding of the supporting infrastructure necessary to deliver serviced plots to the market, taxation (incentives and disincentives), to regulatory issues such as the influence of planning policy and control of development.

4.1 SUPPLY AND DEMAND FOR PLOTS

In contrast to consumer products, property is location specific. This is especially pertinent to market-driven commercial property development, where land value is the most important criterion determining 'what goes where'. According to a comprehensive study published by CABE in 2005, most house buyers will also seek to purchase within a given search area, and consequently supply and demand for

△ Close-grain block plan, Goese Schans,
Goese Diep, the Netherlands
(West 8 Urban Design and Landscape
Architecture)

property may be predetermined by its location rather than its design quality or other characteristics.[64]

4.1.1 Supply

There are a number of factors on the supply side that seem to militate against plot-based development approaches, particularly mixed-use plots:

☐ The property market favours comprehensive single-use developments.

☐ High densities are easier to achieve in medium- or coarse-grain single-use apartment blocks than in close-grain ones.

☐ Narrow plot widths impose technical challenges and higher costs for means of escape and vertical circulation.

☐ There is an inadequate supply of small serviced plots.

☐ The value added by good urban design and architecture is not recognised.

☐ There are challenges arising from tenure.

☐ Institutional inertia.

Property market preferences

Conventional developer-led approaches favour comprehensive development owing to the economies of scale that can be achieved. This usually results in coarse-grain development of blocks for single-use apartments or offices as a whole in the case of brownfield sites, or suburban approaches to mass housing in the case of greyfield and greenfield sites.

A study of mixed uses published by the DCLG points out that single-use development is more favoured by the property market because it is viewed as being more profitable, and a surer investment. Where mixed-use elements are included, they are perceived to signal weak demand, or a hedging of bets in the absence of strong demand for one use over another. Additional uses are sometimes 'bolted on' by developers as a form of planning gain in order to lever concessions from the planning authority. This situation is compounded by mixed-use schemes incorporating residential uses, which normally have lower capital values in town centres than commercial ones.[65]

This conventional model is founded, however, on the concept of property as an investment or as a commodity whose value will continue to rise. The property market crash of 2007 has since raised serious questions about the validity of this assumption. Meanwhile, research by the Prince's Foundation for the Built Environment, also published in 2007, found that the value of new developments characterised by mixed uses, mixed incomes and walkable-scaled neighbourhoods outperformed the conventional model by 18% to 48%.[66] It suggests that this financial attractiveness failed to produce more mixed-use schemes because the conventional business model is ill-equipped to create and manage more complex and diverse schemes, and because fear of the cyclical and unstable nature of the market on the part of developers has led them to extract values as quickly as possible. It now predicts a move back to catering for the needs of homebuyers over investors.

Density

The policy drive towards increased densities on brownfield sites, together with the increased development costs associated with these sites, and growing demand for urban living (at least among younger people and first-time buyers) appears to have compounded the supply-led development of high-density apartment developments in urban areas (where families and older buyers will not consider living) while perpetuating the demand-led development of lower density, but less sustainable, suburban housing developments (where they will).

The middle ground, which is occupied by the potential for low- to medium-rise plot-based development that has the potential to attract mixed uses and families does not seem to have been tapped by developers, with a few exceptions. This is, in large part, due to the fact that close-grain plots cannot achieve comparable densities to medium- or coarse-grain ones owing to the simple economic expedient of having to justify the costs of building high (with lifts) by having a greater number of units per floor to share those costs.

Technical challenges

A study of residual values on behalf of the DCLG comparing hypothetical commercial, residential and mixed-use schemes concluded that (except in peripheral areas) mixed-use schemes are less valuable than single-use ones because their requirements for separate access and circulation, combined with more complicated leasehold arrangements, increase design, construction and management costs.[67] This study noted, however, that the commercial imperative that drives single-use schemes is weaker in peripheral areas and in smaller town centres than in city centres.

Although these conventional development models are more attractive to investors, the relative attractiveness of close-grain mixed-use development (from a purely commercial point of view) improves once certain technical requirements that are invariably applied to large-scale developments, but do not necessarily apply to small-scale ones (such as provision of lifts and basement car-parking), are removed. Crucially, close-grain development also opens up the market to a wider range of smaller developers and investors, whose more short-termist investment criteria and financing arrangements are less constrained than those of their mainstream counterparts or institutional investors.

A residual site value analysis by the author, for example, indicated that up to a height of four or five storeys (beyond which the requirements for lifts and alternative means of escape make going higher less viable for close-grain development plots), the cumulative residual site values achievable by close-grain plots are close on the heels of those for an equivalent hypothetical comprehensive development. Up to this height similar densities are achievable in both forms, meaning that similar site values can also be achieved, provided that the higher cost of development on a plot-by-plot basis can be offset by omitting the requirement for basement parking normally associated with apartment schemes, and provided passenger lifts are not required.

Supply of plots

According to the National Self Build Association (NaSBA), the main factor limiting the growth of self building is the availability of suitable plots in suitable locations.[68] It recommends that masterplans for new towns should incorporate significant provision for self-build plots and that local authorities should identify and provide serviced plots, including through section 106 agreements with developers. It also suggests the need for a public sector agency to assist local authorities in consolidating and re-subdividing sites for sale.

The removal of the national indicative minimum density standard together with the removal of gardens from the definition of previously developed (brownfield) land from PPS3 in 2010 may or may not alleviate overdevelopment of restricted sites. However, it will increase control by planning authorities over the subdivision of gardens to provide for dual occupancy, potentially further reducing the options for small-scale developers and individuals seeking to build on their own behalf.

Recent research by the building agents Savills (October 2010) now supports the view that developer demand for UK residential development land is polarising, with a rift opening up between the value of small, serviced sites, for which demand is strong, and large, strategic regeneration sites and bulk land, which is seeing little trading activity.[69] According to the Prince's Foundation for the Built Environment, there is a question as to whether landowners will sell to developers at prices developers can afford, particularly given the shortage in capital, debt burdens and challenges of funding necessary infrastructure.[70] In contrast, the value of serviced plots and serviceable land is expected to grow over the next few years. This poses a challenge for major landowners to subdivide their holdings into more manageable chunks.

Design

The issue of design is complex, as the cost of good design associated with more challenging layouts, more or better infrastructure, and so on, appears to be more heavily weighted by developers than the benefits. Volume developers in particular seem to resist contemporary or 'unusual' designs on the assumption that this is not what homebuyers want. Studies have shown, however, that good design and quality infrastructure can add value to a scheme. Research conducted on behalf of the north-west regional design review body PlacesMatter! indicates, for example, that good design (including mixed uses) can raise capital and rental values and increase occupancy rates in a challenging market.[71] Unfortunately for architects, however, the appearance of houses seems to be less important to buyers than their location or the attractiveness of the area in general.

Tenure

The traditional mode of development whereby landowners could sell long leases in plots to developers, thereby enabling landowners to control how plots were developed, is challenged now by enfranchisement legislation that allows leaseholders to force the sale of the freehold. This makes it difficult to promote and sustain a regime of long-term estate management that prioritises control of quality and occupation.

According to the Prince's Foundation for the Built Environment, the property market downturn has raised interest in 'built to let' schemes that can stimulate more upfront investment in quality. Tenure remains an issue to potential investors in the case of mixed-use schemes, however, because mixed tenures may hamper the selling on of investments.

Inertia

Most development land in the UK and Ireland is privately owned, and so a system of planning emerged whereby zoning for different land uses operates in tandem with a system of 'development control' (latterly 'development management'). Project proposals generated by the private sector must demonstrate how they 'fit' with the land use and development management objectives set down in the development plan in order to gain consent. Consequently, local authorities in the UK and Ireland are more used to reacting to the market than leading it.

In this context, planning authorities do not have a history or culture of operating as developers or as facilitators of development themselves, or of setting up dedicated delivery organisations mandated and capable of coordinating development proactively rather than reactively.

Added to this, the relative lack of autonomy accorded to local government in the UK and Ireland, its narrow tax base and its corresponding reliance on central government funding means that operating proactively in the development market is perceived as being not merely too difficult, but impossible. This can lead to inertia on the part of the planning authority, which is compounded by the tightly prescribed demarcation of job functions and roles of individuals within it.

In contrast, local authorities in several northern European regions, notably Scandinavia, Germany and the Netherlands, either own a much larger proportion of land or have the means and support to purchase it. This allows the local authority to dictate the terms of development to a far greater extent, because it is, de facto, a development partner in its own right. On this basis, the authority can prepare a masterplan with confidence (rather than asking the developer to do so), and seek tenders from developers to come with

△△ Aerial view of Vathorst, the Netherlands

△ Masterplan of Vathorst, the Netherlands
(West 8 Urban Design and Landscape
Architecture)

a design team consisting of different architects for different plots within a given block. Alternatively, the local authority is in a position to release groups of serviced plots to self builders or building cooperatives.

This single fact of land ownership has been identified by the Scottish Government's study *Delivering Better Places in Scotland*[72] as a critical factor in achieving the much greater degree of diversity found in new developments such as Hammarby in Sweden, Vauban in Germany and Ijburg in the Netherlands.

On the property side, there is a culture divide between those specialising in commercial as opposed to residential development, which seems to perpetuate the tendency to 'bolt-on' additional uses to one or other dominant use rather than try to integrate them properly.[73] This point would also seem to apply to individual self builders, who are primarily concerned with providing a home for themselves, not with property development for its own sake. Small-volume developers, on the other hand, may be more flexible in their approach provided the profitability of the scheme is sufficiently attractive and is adequate to secure funding.

4.1.2 Demand

On the demand side of the equation there is a perception that:

☐ mixed-use street buildings, particularly older stock, do not meet modern needs or expectations

☐ in regard to house type and location, there is a cultural preference for detached and semi-detached houses over flats, and for owning a plot 'from heaven to hell' – that is to say, owning the ground below the plot and the air above it.

According to CABE however:

There are certainly more nuances to home buyers' views than the headlines of market research often suggest. When consumers talk about their aesthetic tastes, most do not like minimalism; but nor do they like the blandness of so much volume house building. They want character; neighbourhoods that feel like places with their own attractive identity. And while they don't like feeling overcrowded, they do value the sorts of local services and sense of community that higher density developments can sustain. Often it is our common associations with the worst of compact living that we reject, rather than the reality of the best. On other questions, home buyers' priorities are very clear. Car-parking obviously remains a huge issue. People don't seem to be happy with solutions that simply put the squeeze on the number of parking spaces in standard housing estates. Yet they might just be prepared to accept smart design to reduce car dependency by creating neighbourhoods that can sustain a good range of local services.[74]

In the case of Vathorst, by West 8, a deliberate decision was taken to supplement what the market demanded with more design-led housing. This has produced a diverse mix of 'classical' and 'contemporary' schemes.[75]

Mixed uses
The presence of shops, schools and local services has been shown by CABE's research to be a major attractant to house buyers. However, many, particularly families with children, are prepared to trade convenience off against a larger house or garden. Similarly, CABE's respondents prefer to be able to walk to local shops and services, as this is perceived to improve the potential for social contact and to engender a sense of community, thereby enhancing a sense of security. But when asked where they would like to live (as opposed to where they actually lived), the responses were tilted towards the countryside.[76]

It has been estimated that there are about 500,000 vacant flats over shops in the UK.[77] This indicates a lack of popularity associated with older mixed-use street buildings. However, their relative affordability combined with the increased popularity of urban living is making them more popular, particularly for first-time buyers availing themselves of stamp duty holidays. The government's recent announcement that consent for change of use from office to residential use will no longer be required may provide some impetus to this.

Other disincentives relate to uncertainty about the breadth of permissible changes of use (e.g. of the ground-floor uses) under the planning acts and the lack of availability of flats with freehold interest.

House type and location

Most people with families, older people and first-time buyers would prefer a detached or semi-detached house for reasons of privacy, security, access and space. In this sense, suburban grass seems greener. Younger people are more willing to opt for terraced housing or flats, in that order. Interestingly, the perception of three-storey townhouses as being impractical owing to the spread of accommodation over three floors had improved in later research cited by CABE, which indicated that the space for children to have their own level, as well as the potential for roof and basement space, is seen as a positive feature of townhouses.

△ Amere's vision for mixed-use blocks

The perception of flats is negatively affected by issues of space, access, privacy and noise, management and, in certain locations, crime. The research is quick to point out, however, that none of these features is inherent to flats as a typology but rather to design, and it attributes this bias to poor design and location in comparison with other countries, where apartment living is more popular.

The relationship of the building to the street is perceived as being particularly important, with most people being resistant to having little or no set-backs from the street on grounds of privacy and the availability of car-parking. There is also a resistance to communal gardens or small gardens, balconies and roof terraces on the part of families with young children.

Clearly, there are design and space-planning issues to be addressed in the quality of development before mainstream perceptions can be changed. The potential of plot-based development as a means of addressing some of these concerns – for example, by providing choice in plot sizes that facilitate a range of house sizes, uses and types, either from a shell pattern that can be adapted to suit individual preferences or by self building – is explored in the Chapter 5. In order to succeed, however, the design of mixed-use street buildings, whether combining live-work, living over the shop or combinations of commercial and apartment dwellings, must also overcome negative perceptions by addressing important design issues such as privacy, security, access, space, storage, construction and communal spaces that are robust and easy to manage. These issues are explored in more detail in Chapter 6.

4.2 OBSTACLES AND OPPORTUNITIES FOR PLOTS

4.2.1 Forward funding

One of the single most significant constraints to close-grain development in general, and plot-based development in particular, arises from the fact that in order for it happen, plots must come to the market 'pre-serviced'. This implies a need for significant upfront investment in infrastructure that neither the public sector nor the private sector is well equipped to deliver on its own. Recent research by Nicholas Falk of UK practice Urbed identifies this as a significant factor in accounting for the ability of the Netherlands to provide higher-quality housing than the UK (measured against Building for Life criteria, for example), citing Dutch arrangements for public-private partnerships to fund advanced infrastructure, develop the masterplan and sell plots to builders.

Case studies prepared on behalf of the Scottish Government [78] suggest the advance provision of social and physical infrastructure matters for a number of related reasons [79]:

☐ It establishes the physical framework for development, thereby demonstrating a commitment to the project.

☐ It provides serviced plots where participants must play by the promoter's rules.

☐ It reduces risk, allowing a greater range of participants to take part, thereby increasing diversity.

☐ It facilitates greater control over phasing and allows projects to proceed at a faster rate.

Property boundaries seldom coincide with masterplans, however, raising the difficulty of reconciling the competing interests of individual property owners with those of the masterplan for the area as a whole. Trying to distribute development land equitably across different landholdings can often compromise the integrity of a masterplan. The landowner saddled with the open-space allocation, for example, can hardly be expected not to be resentful of his neighbour, whose parcel is allocated a more lucrative development land use objective.

An initial process of amalgamation – that is, consolidating plots together so that they can be re-subdivided according to the masterplan – can play an important part in overcoming this problem by providing the means to achieve the desired platting arrangement. This is only likely to happen where either the local authority is the landowner, or a single developer is willing to act in concert with a range of subsidiary parcel or plot developers. In either scenario, the local authority or landowner must also bear the risk of upfront investment in the infrastructure that effectively connects the constituent parcels and plots together for sale later: a factor that can only be mitigated by securing buy-in from the subsidiary parties in advance.

Otherwise, more complex arrangements are required either:

△ **Amalgamating plots as a means of achieving the desired plot subdivision**

☐ to equalise land values across ownership boundaries through re-parcelisation (whereby land ownership is effectively pooled according to share agreements), or

☐ to proportionally allocate development contributions towards supporting infrastructure among the developers who stand to gain from the land being developed.

In some European countries, notably Spain, re-parcelisation is provided for under planning statute, with the express aim of apportioning profits and charges to developers according to their original rights, so that the original ownership pattern can be reconfigured to match the masterplan.

The advance provision of infrastructure in Ijburg in the Netherlands has been likened to the rolling-out of a 'red carpet' where a dedicated delivery organisation (Project Bureau Ijburg) acted to continuously mediate between all of the utility and infrastructure providers. In order to facilitate close-grain plot-based development, the municipality – the City of Amsterdam – not only reclaimed the land itself, but took this one step further by setting out and constructing the piled foundations for individual plots, thereby removing the logistical difficulties of different builders having to operate side by side. The municipality reduced its exposure to risk by entering a public-private partnership whereby it pledged to provide the land and most of the infrastructure, and in return agreed to sell the land at a pre-agreed price.[80]

The community infrastructure levy (CIL)

The community infrastructure levy is a new initiative in England and Wales to fund infrastructure on an area basis with the intention of unlocking land for growth. CIL will supplement, and eventually replace, the current system of planning obligations, which are negotiated on an ad hoc basis through section 106 agreements. Although provision for section 106 agreements will be retained, pooling of section 106 contributions that would be more appropriately funded through CIL will be limited, and they must be more clearly related to the area in which the development is located. They must be[81]:

☐ necessary to make the development acceptable in planning terms

☐ directly related to the development

☐ fairly and reasonably related, in scale and kind, to the development.

CIL will empower local authorities to levy a new charge expressed as a cost per unit, so that it is related to the size and nature of the development, and to expend this locally on supporting infrastructure. Authorities may also apply differential rates to ensure that the levy doesn't prejudice the viability of developments in different areas, for example where land values vary, and may also use the levy to 'backfill' funding provided by another agency or to borrow against future income from the levy. Crucially, a meaningful proportion of the monies raised must be reinvested in the neighbourhood from whence it came. This should make it possible for monies raised through CIL to be ring-fenced for the benefit of locally driven projects and initiatives.

There is clearly potential for CIL in combination with section 106 contributions to advance the development of infrastructure necessary to support the provision of serviced plots either by the local authority or in partnership with developers. However, this efficacy depends on capturing the value added by planning permission and therefore may be curtailed by current economic conditions.

The preparation of Neighbourhood Plans may also provide an opportunity for communities to set their own spending priorities. This could include the parallel provision of ready-to-go plots, together with the social and physical infrastructure to service them, which could then be expedited through Community Right to Build Orders and Neighbourhood Development Orders respectively, without having to go through the conventional planning application process.

Local communities are already taking similar initiatives. The village of Crosby Ravensworth in Cumbria, for example, recently utilised the sale of private building plots – reserved by covenant for local people – to supplement a combination of Homes and Communities Agency (HCA) grant and other funding sources for the construction of affordable housing.[82]

Tax increment financing (TIF)

Tax increment financing empowers local authorities to borrow against predicted future tax revenues, allowing them to capture future uplift in business rates. This procedure has been used successfully for many years in the United States to forward-fund infrastructure, and it is currently being introduced to the UK. It is expected that this will play an important part in regeneration areas designated for the scheme as Accelerated Development Zones (ADZs), particularly as long as revenue streams from developer contributions remain flat.

4.2.2 Taxation

VAT

The dual role of value added tax (VAT) as both an incentive and a disincentive to development is a long-standing issue that was highlighted in the report of the Urban Task Force.

At present there are three rates of VAT on construction:

☐ standard rate (currently 20%)
☐ reduced rate (currently 5%)
☐ zero rate.

The prevailing regime for VAT on construction is described in detail in HM Revenue and Customs Notice 708: Buildings and Construction, November 2011. The rules affecting VAT are extremely complex and subject to frequent change. The following is intended to give an indication of some of the key issues affecting plot-based development, and specialist advice should always be sought.

In general terms, the construction of new dwellings is zero rated, provided the building is designed as a dwelling(s) and its sole use will be residential. A new dwelling may make use of a single façade of a pre-existing building (or two façades on a corner site) and still qualify for zero rating, provided the retention was a requirement of planning permission. Infill houses may also make use of existing party walls shared with neighbouring properties.

An extension to an existing building that creates a new dwelling may also be zero rated, provided the new dwelling is wholly within the extension.

The conversion or renovation of existing buildings for residential use is reduced rated. However, similar work on behalf of a housing association may be zero rated if it involves conversion from a non-residential use or the building has not been in residential use for the previous ten years. Alterations to listed buildings (previously zero rated) are now standard rated.

VAT incurred by self-builders constructing a dwelling may be recovered through the provisions of the DIY House Builders and Convertors VAT Refund Scheme, but only where that VAT has been correctly charged in the first place.

Extensions to existing dwellings that can't be used and sold independently of the main house (such as 'granny flats') are taxed at the full rate, on the grounds that they do not meet the definition of being 'designed as a dwelling'.

A live-work unit is described as a property that combines, within a single unit, a dwelling and commercial or industrial working space as a requirement or condition of planning permission. Zero rating or reduced rating is only available to the extent that the unit comprises the dwelling. Dwellings that contain a home office are not considered to be live-work units and no apportionment is needed. Units where the work area is shown as a discrete area of floor space, be it an office or workshop, must be apportioned to reflect the presence of the commercial element. However, where there is neither a discrete area nor a planning stipulation as to the required percentage of floor area to be used as live-work, no apportionment is required.

In general, the first sale or long lease in a dwelling (including its footprint and a reasonable plot of land around it, and including a dwelling converted from non-residential use or a dwelling not used as such in the previous ten years, but not including a holiday home) is zero rated, whereas the sale of building land – a bare plot – is exempt except where an option to tax has been taken out. This also applies to serviced plots.

In the case of mixed-use buildings, such as a shop with a flat overhead, the zero rating may only be applied to the dwelling. Similarly, where shared infrastructure, such as an access road, serves both zero rated and fully rated construction (e.g. a mixed-use development) the tax liability of the road may be apportioned on a 'fair and reasonable basis' (or otherwise fully rated).

If, however, construction work avails of zero rating on the basis of being for residential use but the use is changed within ten years, then VAT may be payable.

The implications of this for promoting mixed-use developments (including live-work) and also of promoting self-build plots are clear. There is a disincentive to:

- ☐ provide mixed-use street buildings in so far as they may provide for self-contained commercial elements

- ☐ provide dwellings incorporating live-work elements

- ☐ provide for dwellings that are adaptable to commercial use

- ☐ retrofit existing buildings for residential use, as compared to new single-use residential development, except on behalf of Housing Associations

- ☐ retrofit existing buildings for mixed uses, as compared to new single-use residential development

- ☐ the sale of bare plots for mixed-use development, as compared to single-purpose residential use.

The impact of VAT on regeneration projects is highlighted in the case of the retrofitting of older terraced housing stock at Chimney Pot Park, Salford. Here, a greater amount of existing fabric was removed than initially sought by the developer in order to qualify the scheme as 'new build' and thus avoid the higher VAT rate.

A pilot study of the renewal of existing buildings carried out jointly by Dublin City Council and the Heritage Council in Ireland, however, demonstrated that in most circumstances (specifically when refurbishment costs associated with sensitive historic buildings is not too high) retaining and reusing existing buildings on brownfield (i.e. previously developed) sites is more cost effective than redevelopment, with lower whole-life and lower capital costs and reduced environmental impacts per square metre.[83] The difficulty, of course, remains in making such buildings attractive to prospective residents (especially families with children) for the reasons discussed already.

Initiatives to address the disincentive to reuse existing buildings as dwellings have focused on capital allowances such as the 'Living over the Shop' scheme in Ireland. Under this scheme, 100% capital allowances on the costs of refurbishing properties above ground-floor retail and commercial uses for residential use were trialled, albeit with limited success.

Land value taxation

Land value tax (LVT) – a tax on the *potential* value of the plot – has been credited with reducing vacancy in North America and helping to stem the tide of suburbanisation by encouraging developers to make the best use of vacant or under-used land, or to make way for those who will.

LVT is payable regardless of whether or how well the land is actually used. The basic principle of land valuing is that land is valued according to its potential use as defined by the planning authority. Therefore, a land value tax on a site on which a building is permitted would reflect that value. The tax liability remains the same whether or not a plot is utilised in accordance with its planning permission, thus encouraging the plot to be put to its optimal use.

The classical economist Adam Smith included a detailed examination of LVT – which he calls 'ground-rents' – in his seminal work published in 1776, *An Inquiry into the Nature and Causes of the Wealth of Nations*, stating: 'Ground-rents are a still more proper subject of taxation than the rent of houses. A tax upon ground-rents would not raise the rents of houses. It would fall altogether upon the owner of the ground-rent, who acts always as a monopolist, and exacts the greatest rent which he can get for the use of the ground.'[84]

By making it more costly to leave buildings vacant than occupied, LVT would place a financial burden on developers seeking to amalgamate small plots on a piecemeal basis. From the point of view of speculative developers seeking to amalgamate plots for larger projects, this is reason to resist LVT. However, the corollary would be to discourage amalgamation, and the dereliction of existing building fabric that can

△ Aerial view of Chimney Pot Park, Salford: retrofitting of existing terraced housing by Urban Splash (Shed KM Architects)

▽ Sectional perspective showing reconfiguration of typical terraced house at Chimney Pot Park, Salford by Urban Splash (Shed KM Architects)

take place in the intervening period of time, thereby helping to protect close-grain buildings and their underlying plot subdivisions. A secondary effect would be to allow the local authority to recoup some of the cost of infrastructural investment that raises the site's value, such as public transport.

Many of the difficulties associated with implementing LVT arise from the logistics of preparing a comprehensive and accurate cadastral map of plots and their respective owners, together with the methodological issues of valuing land separately from buildings, particularly for mixed-use plots.

Although there is widespread acceptance of the rationale for implementing LVT, the anticipated resistance to it, particularly on the part of financial institutions with vested property interests, means that it is likely to remain on the urbanist's wish list for the foreseeable future. Nevertheless, further investigation is warranted to see whether it could be implemented selectively in vulnerable areas alongside protective measures to incentivise redevelopment of plots and reuse of underused or vacant upper floors in inner urban areas.

4.2.3 Regulatory issues

Planning law and building regulations in England and Wales are set down by the UK parliament in the form of primary legislation (the planning acts) and subordinate legislation (statutory instruments). Scotland, Northern Ireland and the Republic of Ireland have their own planning acts, their own building regulations and their own planning policy. Planning policy for Wales is also devolved. The devolution of power to the Welsh Assembly Government (WAG) means, however, that much of the planning legislation relating to England and Wales is applied differentially. To complicate the situation, the WAG has legislative competence in certain matters, while other matters are carried forward on a joint England and Wales basis.

In many respects, however, the planning systems in England, Wales, Scotland, Northern Ireland and the Republic of Ireland operate in a similar way: they all comprise a system of development plans, development management and enforcement. They all express planning policy outside of the legislative framework and, most importantly for the purposes of this book, the objectives of urban design apply to them equally.

What England, Wales, Northern Ireland and the Republic of Ireland also have in common is that they are common law jurisdictions, whereas Scots law has its roots in several different systems, including common law and Roman law. This has some implications for property and land-use planning. Law 'grows in the hands of the judges' and so, unless stated to the contrary, where it is necessary for this book to refer to legislative or regulatory matters, it focuses on the situation pertaining to England and Wales, with reference to equivalent provisions in Ireland and Northern Ireland.

The plot is not afforded any regulatory protection under the planning acts. Buildings and structures of interest can be listed for protection, and areas of architectural or heritage interest may be designated for special protection. However, the plots on which buildings sit have very limited and indirect status.

The principal means by which close-grain plot subdivisions survive is by virtue of the buildings that occupy them or are situated next to them. Once these buildings are removed, the obstacle to the plots' amalgamation is also removed. Although the character of a conservation area – which frequently derives from a close grain of buildings and plots – is a material consideration in any new development proposal, it is usually the appearance of the proposed replacement in relation to its close-grain neighbours that is the determining factor, and not the underlying plot subdivision. Consequently, redevelopment that appears to follow the grain is often permitted even though what appears to be two or more buildings is really one building. These kinds of buildings give a superficial impression of variety through the manipulation

△△ Plan of Bachelor's Walk, Dublin:
single-aspect apartment blocks
accessed via a central spine corridor

△ The façade of the blocks is manipulated
to give the appearance of a close-grain
plot subdivision

of their façades, but they do not share the same potential for generating diversity as individual buildings on separate plots.

A requirement to obtain planning permission for the subdivision and amalgamation of plots (as is required in some other countries, e.g. Australia) would allow the planning authority to consider the effects of subdivision on future development in terms of urban grain and its potential to foster diversity. Protecting close-grain plot subdivisions in heritage areas would allow sensitive infill to take place that would be more sustainable in the long term than its 'façadist' alternative.

As concluded by the DCLG's study of mixed uses:

> We observe a paradox that … tends to view mixed-use development as a problematic new development product, yet we can see the effortless legacy of mixed-use development areas throughout our cities and towns. Given the apparent difficulty in creating a similar fine grain mix of uses … we should do the utmost to safeguard and enhance existing quality mixed-use environments.[85]

Control of development in the UK and Ireland is regulated through the planning acts. Under the acts, the local planning authority has considerable discretion to take into account a wide range of 'material considerations' in deciding whether or not to grant permission. These include the provisions of the statutory development plan, planning policy and a wide range of technical and aesthetic considerations upheld by the courts. This discretion, which operates at the time the decision is made, distinguishes the UK and Irish systems from those of many other countries, where the decision is effectively made when the development plan is adopted. The principal implication of this for plot-based urbanism is that, in contrast to countries where development is 'as of right' provided it complies with the plan, the development of individual plots can only proceed on a piecemeal basis as and when individual applications are granted.

There are four ways to circumvent this under the current system:

- ☐ outline planning permission
- ☐ design codes
- ☐ Local Development Orders
- ☐ Neighbourhood Development Orders (England only).

Suffice to say that the potential for these powers to be used for better or worse lies in the balance and, as suggested by former RIBA president Ruth Reed, the potential for architects to tip the scales in favour of good design is up for grabs.[86]

The significance of outline planning permission is that it determines the acceptability in principle of proposed development on the basis of relatively basic information: the proposed uses, indicative layout and scale parameters. Details of reserved matters for approval may be submitted together or separately for different parts of the site – that is, for individual plots.[87] Thus a plot-based masterplan may be submitted for outline planning permission to determine the location and heights of buildings spread over the area of the masterplan, in advance of detailed designs for separate plots. The disadvantage with this is that detailed approvals must fall within the scope of the outline permission and be sought within the life of the outline grant.

Incorporating a similar range and scope of information about plots, building types, footprints and heights into a design code can effectively front-load the time spent in the development control process in a similar way, thus streamlining decision-making on individual applications that follow the code. Where they exist, compliance with the design code is often required by the landowner, and subject to legal agreement between the parties. Design codes may also be adopted as Supplementary Planning Guidance (SPGs), provided that they are compliant with national and local policy, making them a material consideration for development control purposes. On this point, CABE notes that the degree to which the code has been subject of consultation will significantly affect the weight accorded to it by the planning authority.[88] Design codes may also be given status through planning conditions or planning agreements; and, in some cases, if the code has been adopted by the elected members, a planning application may be decided through delegated powers.[89] In Ireland, design codes are not in widespread use; however, masterplans that incorporate equivalent detailed urban design guidance relating to the area covered by the masterplan are commonly adopted by the planning authority as Local Area Plans (LAPs) or as variations to the development plan.

Local Development Orders (LDOs) were brought in to help speed up the planning process by allowing local planning authorities to extend permitted development rights for a type or form of development specified in the order, thus removing the need to apply for permission. The LDO can be applied to the entire administrative area or to a single site. Similar provisions operate in Simplified Planning Zones (SPZs). According to the Planning Advisory Service (PAS), the LDO may be cross-referenced with a masterplan or a design code, and therefore one of the principal opportunities afforded by LDOs is to enable masterplanned development.[90]

Equivalent powers in Irish legislation provide Strategic Development Zones (SDZs), wherein basic information set out in the form of a detailed masterplan (termed a 'planning scheme') with accompanying guidance relating to, for example, land uses or building lines and height, are set out. Once the planning scheme has been adopted, development proposals that comply with it must be approved. Part of the attraction of LDOs and SPZs (and SDZs) was thus to speed up the approvals process, but they have not proved popular with planning authorities.

Neighbourhood Development Orders (NDOs) are based on the same idea as LDOs, but the power to make them is devolved (in England) to local communities. This will provide a major (as yet untried) opportunity to enable plot-based development for small-scale housing and/or mixed-use developments. Once a Neighbourhood Development Plan (NDP) has been adopted by the community, the NDO can be used to bypass the local authority requirement to obtain planning permission. The NDP may be used to set out plots and basic parameters for their use, footprint and height, which could present a major opportunity for alternative development models to advance unfettered by current requirements.

4.3 ALTERNATIVE DEVELOPMENT MODELS

4.3.1 Strategic land investment model

This model focuses on partnering between developers and landowners as a means of facilitating a more sophisticated approach to place-making. The concept, promoted by the Prince's Foundation for the Built Environment, recognises the limitations of the conventional business model that favours single-use development by volume developers. In particular, it identifies the fragility of the conventional development model, which, it argues, arises from its dependence on a rising market and realising cash receipts as early as possible in the process. The Foundation also highlights the failure of the conventional model to produce sustainable mixed-use, mixed-tenure developments.

The significance of this for plot-based urbanism is that it puts in place the infrastructure necessary to release serviced plots to the market on a phased basis, and thus allows development to take place in a more incremental fashion than comprehensive development, where all the infrastructure and buildings are constructed at once.

The Foundation's Strategic Land Investment Model (SLIM) suggests that the current impasse caused by developers unable to raise finance or meet their existing agreements with landowners can be unlocked by partnering landowners with developers, and by de-coupling land promotion – the laying out of plots for sale on an incremental and phased basis – from development as a single activity.[91] It argues that this approach can ease cash flow in the early stages while sustaining a longer-term view of investment that (providing onerous tax disincentives are not imposed on landowners) can provide confidence that investment can be recouped later when the market recovers, and help unlock the provision of supporting infrastructure.

In this model, unlocking value is realised through masterplanning, infrastructure delivery and long-term management, instead of through planning permission, so that the sale of plots is phased to capture rising value. Land interest remains in the scheme as equity, allowing the landowners to benefit from uplift, and allowing investment to be focused on supporting infrastructure. Achieving this requires a partnering arrangement between the promoter and the landowner, who maintain a long-term interest and enforce quality through contractual mechanisms.

The promoter's initial investment in masterplanning and promotion is rewarded through receipts from early land sales. Capital is not required from the landowner but their interest is vested (on an equalised basis in the case of multiple landowners) so that they are able to retain the use of the land for other purposes until it is required and participate in the uplift in value arising from planning permission, and can sell their stake to raise cash if needed. Long-term investment is required from the investor in infrastructure.

A similar model is operated in France, where a public-private (not for profit) vehicle is established by affiliated planning authorities to buy land at its pre-existing use value, provide infrastructure and recoup the investment from the sale of parcels or plots to different developers.

4.3.2 Self building

Self building usually means one of three things:

- ☐ a private person employing an architect and building contractor

- ☐ a private person employing an architect and managing the build

- ☐ a private person employing a kit-house supplier to design and build.

Thus, except where the owner actually builds the house themselves, investing 'sweat equity', self building is more accurately termed self procurement.

The significance of self building for plot-based urbanism is that the self build industry as a whole adds up to a significant demand for individual development plots. In each case, the individual self builder must find a suitable serviced (or serviceable) plot of land.

According to the National Self Build Association (NaSBA), most self builders in the UK are couples approaching retirement who wish to build their dream home, younger people who wish to save money, or entrepreneurs. The NaSBA now attributes a tenfold increase in self build house completions (from 2,000 thirty years ago) to 20,000 in 2008 to rising demand, making the output of this segment second only to volume house builder Taylor Wimpey.[92]

The scale and economic significance of the self build sector has received Government recognition in its Housing Strategy for England. Published in November 2011, the strategy (which refers to the 'custom build' industry), asks Councils to establish the demand for custom build housing in their area and to take positive steps to facilitate it. Swindon Borough Council has taken the lead by approving the sale of a former primary school site at Windmill Hill for a self build scheme comprising 12 self build house plots, with potential for a further 13 plots. It is intended that full permission for the houses will be granted, which can then be modified by the self builders within the parameters set by a design code. The Council (in partnership with self build specialists Build-Store), has reduced its exposure to risk in this instance by undertaking to construct the supporting infrastructure (roads and utilities) once prospective self builders are under contract to purchase all of the plots. At the time of writing, this is believed to be the first instance of so called 'enabled self procurement' (ESP) occurring in the UK.

The municipality of Almere has tapped into a latent demand for self building in the Netherlands by providing whole swathes of self-build serviced plots where individuals are given free rein to unleash their individual creativity. The municipality suggests that this model has proved remarkably resistant to the economic downturn because it has put in place links with specific funding providers and because many prospective purchasers are using their personal savings to finance building. According to the Housing Strategy for England, "Almere demonstrates a genuinely workable model for large scale, locally led and affordable self build development…"[93]

4.3.3 Building cooperatives

Building cooperatives are a form of self building, whereby a group of like-minded individuals or families come together to purchase a site with the intention of self building as a group. They typically comprise self-selected groups of up to 20 families who are attracted by the idea of influencing the design of their own home. There is a significant precedent for development by building cooperatives in Germany, notably in Vauban and Freiburg, and in Almere Poort, near Amsterdam.

Building cooperatives do not typically have an overt social agenda but they do foster a community building spirit and, by virtue of building on small plots together, facilitate genuinely diverse and varied results. A particular benefit of this model from the point of view of promoting plot-based

urbanism is that building cooperatives come to the market with the specific aim of cooperating. Their willingness to work together thus helps to overcome some of the main problems associated with different builders working cheek by jowl, particularly where neighbouring construction projects share plot boundaries.

In the case of Vauban, a masterplan was prepared by the local authority and plots were allocated preferentially to building co-ops (*Baugruppen*), with bids assessed against a range of criteria favouring families with children, older people and local residents.[94] It is noteworthy, however, that the *Baugruppen* needed significant support from the local authority, which set up a technical support unit, increasing start-up time.[95] A special company (Buergerbau AG) was established to help coordinate and manage all the building cooperative groups. This company assisted in putting the groups together, providing guidance and information to the group throughout the process, and managing costs, quality control, finance and accounting.[96]

4.3.4 Co-housing

Co-housing is another form of self building; however, most co-housing groups have a social and/or environmental agenda of some kind. This often takes the form of a shared space, such as a community centre, shared infrastructure, such as heating systems, and shared activities, such as home-based agriculture or community meals, as well a commitment to forming an intentional community. Most co-housing groups own their own houses and vet incoming residents with a view to building a diverse yet balanced community.

Co-housing groups where houses are privately owned are usually set up as joint venture private companies. Each member must make a minimum investment in shares, and individuals may purchase their own home from the company. The company then assumes responsibility for any rental elements and the shared facilities, for which members

△ Modern close-grain townhouses, Vauban, Freiburg, Germany

◁ View of the shared open space at 'The Yard', Ashley Vale, Bristol

pay a service charge. There is also scope for co-housing groups to partner with a housing association or to become one themselves. This has advantages such as access to grant funding and management, making it easier to provide afford-able rents, but with reduced control over design, location and who can join.

According to the UK Cohousing Network, there are ten fully established co-housing communities in the UK, with a fur-ther 25 to 30 in formation.[97]

'The Yard', Ashley Vale, is an interesting example that com-bines several elements of both self building and co-housing on an infill brownfield (former industrial) site in Bristol. The Yard includes some 20 self-build plots, a group of six self-finished bungalows and six self-finished apartments, a small number of work spaces and a community/shared space, loosely arranged around a communal green space.

Although there are a variety of house types and sizes, as well as an element of mixed use, it is noteworthy that the self-build elements of the project are predominantly detached houses. This minimised the logistical difficulty faced by indi-vidual self builders having to coordinate their design and building work with adjoining plots.

One of the principal advantages of these forms of development taken together is that they pre-empt the 'short-termism' inherent in conventional forms of developer-led speculative development. Construction costs for self builders are lower overall (around 30% according to the NaSBA) and the balance between the upfront capital costs of low energy design and operating costs is more attractive.

This means that, provided supporting infrastructure can be provided in advance, and provided investors can be per-suaded to take a longer-term view of their investment, plot-based urbanism has the potential to create a win–win for the consumer, the developer, the landowner and the local planning authority. For the consumer, it is realised in buildings that are simultaneously more suited to their needs and more affordable, with better access to local services. For the devel-oper/landowner, value is added through the masterplanning process, as well as by good design, and a portion of risk is transferred. For the planning authority, slow release of plots and/or parcels helps to stabilise the local property market because controlling the supply of plots and development of plots helps to maintain demand over a sustained period. For whoever forward-funds the infrastructure, however, whether it is the landowner, the developer or the local authority, greater risk is entailed upfront but there is the potential to reap higher returns in the medium to longer term.

Against this backdrop, the current UK policy and practice of identifying the amount of development land needed to service projected demand and then adding a percentage in the hope that this will stimulate competition seems, at best, flawed.

4.4   KEY STAKEHOLDERS

Case studies of recent developments that have succeeded in generating diversity, conducted on behalf of the Scottish Government,[98] indicate that they tend to share one or more of the following characteristics:

- ☐ good designers
- ☐ a 'project champion'
- ☐ a proactive local authority
- ☐ a dedicated project delivery team
- ☐ an enlightened developer, and/or
- ☐ an enlightened client.

4.4.1 The designer

CABE's *Creating Successful Masterplans*, first published in 2004, emphasises that, ultimately, it is people with the right talents who deliver great projects. Although this could be said to apply across the whole project team, it is to the designer that the team and its client look first for vision, direction and design quality.

The role of the designer is pivotal in several key areas throughout the masterplanning process, and should not be underestimated:

☐ developing the client's brief

☐ setting up the project, assessing the need for other consultants and coordinating a diverse range of inputs

☐ acting as the point of client contact and as the interface between the client and other stakeholders

☐ developing a thorough understanding of the place

☐ agreeing a vision for what the place will be like, communicating it effectively to others and securing 'buy-in' from stakeholders

☐ generating strategies and hierarchies for urban and landscape structure, function and land uses, movement and access, etc.

☐ creating integrated urban design frameworks

☐ providing detailed design guidance on key streets and spaces, height, scale and massing of buildings, building typologies and urban grain, etc.

☐ guiding delivery.

In all these areas, the designer can motivate others to achieve the extraordinary over the ordinary, if they play a proactive role in joining what the Scottish Government terms the 'coalition' of support for the project. It goes on to suggest that in order to have a catalytic effect design consultants should be 'value-positive' rather than 'value-neutral': a distinction which it attributes to an ethos or mindset that transcends discipline or qualification.

The architect's role in the design, coordination and administration of ever more complex building projects has tended to be eroded by the inclusion of specialist professionals, such as project managers and surveyors, for example. But there remains in the arena of urban design a central role for the architect in ensuring that the emerging masterplan and proposals are continuously tested against the vision, and, above all, will produce successful places. The designer is best placed to avoid the scope creep that can arise from the involvement of other disciplines whose mindset and project focus is frequently more concerned with 'development' than with 'place'.

Perhaps the biggest challenge facing the designer (and architecture as a profession) in promoting a plot-based approach to masterplanning, however, is that it implies de-coupling masterplanning from the design and procurement of the buildings themselves, and allowing a greater range of different designers and developers to contribute. This, in turn, requires an acceptance that place-making happens over much longer time horizons than individual building projects and, as such, is bigger than any single architect. This will involve a culture shift away from the concept of 'starchitect' as omni-influential visionary creator, to accepting the more humble role of facilitator in the first instance and, subsequently, accepting the role of contributor to the plurality of urban fabric.

The municipality of Almere near Amsterdam is currently coordinating Europe's largest experiment in plot-based development. Located in Almere Poort, the project was masterplanned by OMA but is being driven and coordinated by the municipality, with Jacqueline Tellinga at the helm. Drawing on the example of a similar plot-based development in Tübingen, Germany, the municipality actively promotes architects as key drivers who initiate and generate ideas and translate them into a concrete design.[99]

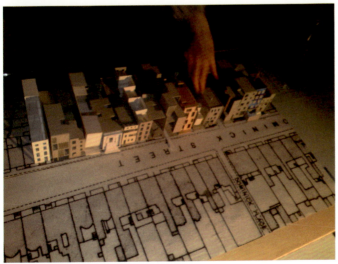

△ Preliminary model for close-grain mixed-use block in Almere Poort, the Netherlands

◁ Ideas competition for close-grain town houses, Dominick Street, Dublin, instigated by Dublin City Council

This will reduce the potential for larger practices to simultaneously both determine the masterplan and hoover up large chunks of the resulting development, but will have commensurate benefits for the involvement of smaller practices, who are better placed to invest care in the design of its smaller constituent parts. In principle, promoting the diversity of participants at every level should improve the health of the profession as a whole.

4.4.2 The project champion

'Project champion' is not an official title, but the term has come into common usage to describe someone who takes on the task of promoting a place or project. Experience shows that the project champion can make a vital contribution to getting a project off the ground that might otherwise languish in obscurity. The need for a project champion is most pressing in relation to projects that are in some way innovative or out of the ordinary, because their uniqueness makes them difficult for established institutions or procedures to deal with.

In this context, case studies examined by the Scottish Government have concluded that the support of a high-level, influential person is a decisive success factor shared by a range of innovative projects across the UK and Europe that are widely lauded as 'best practice' exemplars. A case in point is the Hammarby-Sjöstad area of Stockholm, Sweden – renowned for its ecological credentials and the diversity and range of its participants – which is largely credited to Stockholm's chief architect/planner, Jan Inge-Hagström.[100]

Ideally, the project champion will be a dynamic individual within a supportive organisation who has the drive and influence to generate a compelling vision for a place, galvanise support for it across diverse sectoral interests and motivate others to implement it. The project champion is often a professional acting within the local authority, such as an architect, urban designer or town planner, or a private sector individual.

Plot-based urbanism is not the norm in the UK and Ireland, but awareness and support for it is growing. For example, Dublin City Architect Ali Grehan recently instigated a competition to generate interest in regenerating a street in the city with individual close-grain plots. So it is likely that the vision and support of individuals like this may prove crucial to the implementation of such projects here, at least until it enters the mainstream.

4.4.3 The local authority

Often the public sector, as the statutory authority, must provide the necessary leadership in order to attract investment from the private sector. The local authority is tasked with reconciling private interests with the interests of the common good. This enables it to take a longer-term view than the private sector, but also requires it to do so. The capability of the local authority to drive the diversity agenda is significantly enhanced when it is also the landowner. Unfortunately, this is not usually the case in the UK or Ireland, and in order to compensate, local planning authorities need to be more proactive in garnering support for plot-based approaches among other key stakeholders, especially landowners and developers.

Many local authorities lack in-house urban design or architectural skills, however, reducing the likelihood of their being able to identify and promote suitable development opportunities. The lack of education and/or training in design on the part of town planners, the public and elected representatives in particular can also lead to misguided or ill-informed interference by the local authority in privately driven initiatives, to the detriment of the design quality or feasibility of a masterplan or project. This can waste time and resources, result in unnecessary compromise and, as a result, place a strain on professional relationships. In certain circumstances, especially where an impasse between the local authority and the project proponent appears to be developing, it may be in the interests of both parties to participate in design review.

Design review is a service free to local authorities, developers and designers that gives impartial advice on development proposals at the pre-planning stage. Design review panels are typically composed of a range of highly qualified and experienced design professionals, and although it is not mandatory for either party to take account of their views, the weight accorded to them by the local planning authority can generate confidence in the design quality of the scheme and galvanise the coalition of support for it. Preferably, design review should be undertaken when there is enough work done to enable a meaningful discussion to take place, yet early enough to ensure that potentially abortive work is avoided, and that a consensus can be reached as to the best way forward.

The National Planning Policy Framework expects local planning authorities to have local design review arrangements in place to provide assessment and support to ensure high standards of design and, when appropriate, refer major projects for a national design review (currently provided by the Design Council and CABE).

Local authorities are therefore in a strong position to harness the expertise available through design review to influence the direction of significant schemes at an early stage of the design process, helping to ensure that, where appropriate and beneficial, they can generate close-grain diversity and mixed uses.

4.4.4 The project delivery team

Especially for large or complex sites, leadership at the strategic level is not enough, and must be complemented by a dedicated team that can activate and maintain the necessary dialogue to secure delivery of diversity on the ground. This can take the form of a special in-house team within the local authority or an external public, private or public-private partnership arrangement:

- [ ] a local authority or public agency that acts as land developer facilitating multiple developers

- [ ] a delivery agent who, through consolidated land transfer, acts as land developer with multiple developers

- [ ] an 'enlightened' developer or consortium who acts as land developer with multiple developers.

Within any project delivery team, the designer should strive to play a central role in promoting design quality and place-making.

4.4.5 The developer

In the UK and Ireland – where there is a less strong place-shaping culture than in some other European countries, coupled with lower levels of public ownership of development land and limited resources – some of the most innovative and diverse developments have come from the private sector. The 'enlightened developer' is a term coined by the Scottish Government[101] to describe a land developer as a promoter, who acts in conjunction with multiple parcel developers, and to distinguish those developers who, in doing so, prioritise place quality and diversity above short-term maximisation of their own capital receipts.

The Scottish Government's study highlights the role of the developer of Harlow in Essex, for example, which adopted a more 'patient capital' approach to development whereby the capital receipts for phase 2 of the development were higher than those for phase 1, as a result of the higher quality and subsequent demand that phase 1 generated.

There is increasing pressure on developers (and acceptance on the part of a few) that so-called 'Lego-land' developments, characterised by single-use 'identikit' housing, are no longer acceptable and that they must look to urban designers and architects to deliver quality and diversity through the masterplanning process.

It is in the interests of the designer (and built environment professionals generally) to draw the attention of their clients, especially developers, to the potential 'win–win' that achieving the objectives of good urban design, especially mixed uses, mixed housing and variety at the masterplanning stage, can bring to the success of their projects. One way of doing this is to highlight examples of good places elsewhere, and, if it's practical to visit them, arrange with the client to do so.

4.4.6 The client

In most circumstances, clients are public agencies (or quasi-public agencies), private developers (or consortia of developers) or community groups. By definition, however, the eventual clients for diverse plot-based developments, are likely to comprise a diverse range of groups and individuals who are also the end-users. In some cases, the client may comprise a group of self builders or a co-housing cooperative, which may share a vision for developing individual houses and shared facilities together.

This raises the issue that the client can, and often does, change as the masterplanning process moves through different stages from inception to implementation. There is a marked tendency for the understanding of who the 'client' is to shift from the narrower definition of instigator/paymaster, to that of the residents and the wider community, or 'the place' itself.

The designer can also change – and it is in the interests of generating diversity to introduce a range of different designers and developers at more detailed design stages. But the masterplanner faces the not inconsiderable challenge of balancing the client's needs and expectations with those of the local authority, developers, the local community and the exigencies of good practice in urban design while also protecting and enhancing the positive qualities of the place itself.

Building cooperatives can implement diverse schemes more easily and quickly than self builders purchasing bare plots on an ad hoc basis, because they have in place an organisational structure to facilitate coordination of shared elements such as party walls and community infrastructure such as district heating or open space. They can also benefit from economies in scale from the bulk purchase of building materials, but they require their own 'project champion', their own mini delivery team and their own designers.

△ Model of proposed close-grain street of townhouses, 'Tutti Frutti', New Islington, Manchester, by Urban Spash (various architects)

▷ Judging the model

5 Designing the plot

5.1 STRATEGIC APPROACHES TO DESIGNING DIVERSITY

Designing diversity is a contradiction in terms: how can something genuinely diverse be designed without being contrived? The extent to which a given development will attract a range of different developers (and, in turn, different designers) is in large part a product of the degree to which the masterplan for the development is subdivided into parcels, blocks or plots. Similarly, the size of developer attracted will be affected by the size of the parcel, block or plot. The finer the grain of development provided for in the masterplan, the greater the range and diversity of developers that can participate and, in turn, the greater the degree of diversity in terms of uses, types and tenures that can be generated. So the answer lies not in designing *per se*, but in creating the conditions – including a diverse range of parcel, block and plot sizes and shapes – within which a diverse range of designers and interests can flourish and adapt to changing circumstances over time.

In this sense, the laying out of close-grain serviced plots is akin to the deliberate sinking of a ship onto a hitherto featureless seabed. Just as the ship forms a ready-made reef onto which the myriad of corals, anemones and sea creatures can attach themselves to create a new ecosystem, subdivided blocks form a substrate on which different self builders and lower-volume developers can realise their own

individual development programmes and, ultimately, create the conditions necessary to sustain a more diverse web of social and economic interaction and street life.

Of course, this is an overly simplistic analogy. The layout, configuration and size of blocks and their subdivision into plots must be robust enough to adapt to different circumstances and to change over time, and, above all, must be tailored to suit the nature and extent of diversity that is both desirable and feasible in any given context. In addition, it may be necessary for the rules of the game – building lines, massing, height – to be predefined, and protocols for the interfaces between plots – such as building on boundaries – to be established.

At the strategic level, each of the following approaches is likely to achieve a successively greater measure of diversity compared with comprehensive development over a wider area:

☐ the allocation of *individual blocks* to different developers

☐ the allocation of *parts of blocks* to different developers, including co-housing groups or building cooperatives

☐ the allocation of *individual plots within blocks* to different developers, including building cooperative groups and/or self builders.

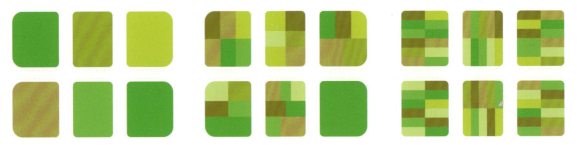

△ Strategic subdivision options

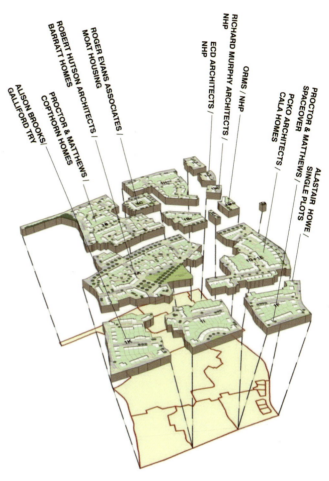

Hybrids of these options are also possible where, for example, control of a single block (or blocks) may be retained by one developer but where different architects are commissioned to design buildings for individual plots. Further possibilities include commissioning a variety of building designs by different designers to fit a predefined plot size that are then distributed, or developing several plots together as building shells and then inviting a range of different architects to design façades and fit-outs.

A UK example of the first approach – allocating blocks to different developers/design teams – is located in Newhall, Harlow in Essex.

The size of development parcels is typically 50 to 200 dwellings but there are also smaller parcels and individual building plots. According to the masterplanners, Studio REAL, the key design principle is that the greatest diversity of architects should be around the most prominent public spaces. Working from home is encouraged throughout the neighbourhood and on streets adjacent to local centres. Higher ceiling heights and provision of a separate access off the street are required in order to make dwellings capable of accommodating a small business.

There is also a planning requirement to provide 2 ha of employment, but rather than provide this as a single land use, the equivalent number of jobs is being delivered through mixed-use development focused around the local and future district centre.

Schemes where parts of blocks are allocated to different developers are commonplace in France and Sweden.[102] Again, this approach depends on a masterplan being prepared and plots sold on to different developers. In

△ Studio workshops at Newhall, Harlow
(Studio REAL)

△ Allocation of development parcels to
different design teams at Newhall,
Harlow (Studio REAL)

France, the mechanism for achieving this is the Zone d'Aménagement Concerté (ZAC). The ZAC is a comprehensive and integrated delivery vehicle for land acquisition, masterplanning and provision of infrastructure.[103] Implementation of the ZAC is carried out by not-for-profit agencies called SEMs (Societé d'Economie Mixte), which are composed of a range of public and private shareholders. In France, land assembly is aided by the right of the state to buy land at its pre-existing use value. One such example of two developers operating within the same block is found in Parc Richter, Montpellier. It is noteworthy in this case that the two halves of the U-shaped blocks are not joined together, because this reduces logistical problems during design and construction phases of development.

The third strategic approach – allocating individual plots within blocks to developers – has been pioneered by the city of Tübingen in Germany for the Südstadt area. Other examples are found in Vauban in Freiburg (Germany), Ijburg, on the outskirts of Amsterdam, and Almere Poort, near Amsterdam (the Netherlands). With the exception of Almere Poort, however, which is currently in progress, these have not achieved the same level of vertical mixed uses as in Tübingen Südstadt.

In Tübingen Südstadt, a masterplan was developed following a competition-winning proposal by Büro LEHEN drei in 1993. The project is being realised as a *Städtebauliche Entwicklungsmaßnahme*, which means that the city buys the site, undertakes necessary planning and then sells the plots to private builders. Housing for 6,500 residents and commercial units providing for about 2,000 new jobs are expected to be completed before the end of 2015. The project is coordinated by the *Stadtsanierungsamt* (Municipal Office for Revitalisation), with support from private consultants (including Büro LEHEN drei) and other contractors.

The *Stadtsanierungsamt* identifies the following six elements as being key to the success of the project.[104]

Small-parcelled mixed use

The desegregation of living and working is identified as rendering the organisation of daily life easier, facilitating contacts and minimising distances. The objective was to create a small-parcelled, vertical mixture of compatible uses (as of 2004, around 160 businesses with about 900 employees had decided to settle there).

Provision of social and cultural infrastructure

Within the framework of the masterplan, a wide variety of public, social and cultural facilities have been created to serve the Südstadt, as well as the wider area. The city has invested about 15 million euros, generated by the sale of plots, into kindergardens, day-care facilities, schools and other community facilities.

Density and the reuse of existing buildings

Building density is exceptionally high in the Südstadt. In addition to general sustainability considerations, this has allowed the development to be kept affordable to a broad cross-section of people from different socio-economic backgrounds.

Building cooperatives and parcelling-out

The majority of the Südstadt homeowners are private builders who have joined together in *Baugruppen* (private building cooperatives). This has fostered the creation of a multitude of very different, highly individual projects, most of them with much lower costs than those generated by conventional builders. This is made possible by consistently selling the plots to private bidders, by determining the size and shape of each plot in accordance with the buyer's needs and by a supportive city administration.

Social mixing

The Südstadt has been settled by a diverse cross-section of the population, including senior citizens, non-nationals, disabled people and students. The municipality attributes this to the involvement of building cooperatives.

△ Extract from block plan for Tübingen Südstadt, showing plot subdivisions

◁ Corresponding view of part of close-grain block facing new square

Public space, traffic and civic participation

The function of the Südstadt's public realm as a traffic network has been relegated to second place, with priority given over to walking and cycling. Cars are not prohibited; however, the vehicles of employees, inhabitants and visitors are parked in public neighbourhood garages.

The first hybrid-type approach to creating variety – sprinkling a wide variety of house designs throughout the area – is illustrated here by two West 8 projects, in Vathorst and Ypenburg, both in the Netherlands. An earlier example of this approach is Borneo Sporenburg in Amsterdam, also masterplanned by West 8. This approach has been characterised by Campbell as 'bar-code' urbanism.[105] This is a somewhat disparaging characterisation made on the basis that different building designs are repeated. Nevertheless, both schemes display a genuine attempt to relieve monotony by proving a range of different designs, and in the case of Borneo

◁ Kai Park, Vathorst, Amersfoort, the Netherlands (West 8 Urban Design and Landscape Architecture)

△ Residential perimeter block, Ypenburg, the Netherlands (West 8 Urban Design and Landscape Architecture)

▷ Interior view of a courtyard block with individually designed façades (Arkitema Architects)

▷▷ Concept diagram by Arkitema Architects illustrating potential for design of façades by different architects

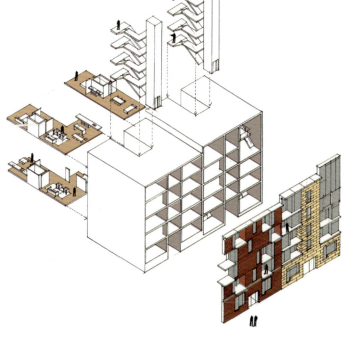

Sporenburg, a wide range of different architects were used. Psychologist Dr Paul Keedwell suggests this variety meets an aesthetic need for complexity within order and vice versa.[106]

Lastly, the example of Sluseholmen in Copenhagan (Denmark), by Arkitema, shows how variety has been created through inviting a range of different architects to design individual façades and internal fit-outs to 'pre-made' building shells. Again, this results in the appearance of variety, which it could be argued is only 'skin deep'. On the other hand, this approach has overcome the issues associated with accommodating different designers in the same block, while also facilitating genuine variety both in the appearance of the apartments that make up the block and in their interior architecture.

5.2 PROMOTING SUSTAINABLE DENSITIES

One of the principal challenges facing the development of close-grain plots is achieving densities that are high enough to make them sustainable in terms of their efficient use of land, infrastructure and services compared with other typologies. As outlined in Chapter 4, for example, there are a number of constraints relating to vertical circulation that make it more difficult to achieve very high densities as compared with other block typologies. These constraints effectively conspire to limit the scale of close-grain plots to four or five storeys, where lift access and/or alternative means of escape isn't feasible. It is argued that, paradoxically, its relatively low scale is one of the features of traditional close-grain development that makes it more humane, and thus more attractive to people in the long term. However, this needs to be balanced with broader sustainability objectives, especially the viability of mixed uses. The overall objective of achieving high densities thus needs to take

Urban grain and density:

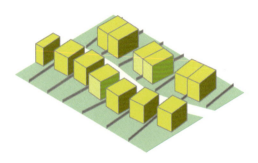

△ Close-grain suburban (low-rise linear or dendritic pattern); Indicative density: 15–20 units per hectare; Diversity level: low.

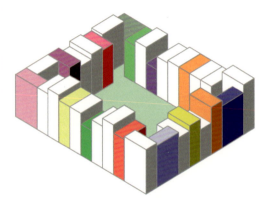

△ Close-grain urban (medium-rise perimeter block); Indicative density: 55–70 units per hectare; Diversity level: high.

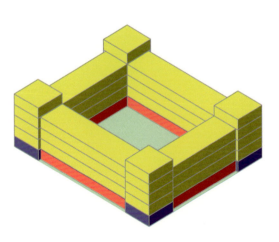

△ Medium to coarse-grain urban (medium-rise perimeter block); Indicative density: 55–70 units per hectare; Diversity level: low to medium.

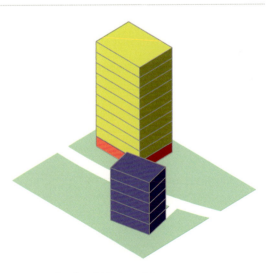

△ Coarse-grain urban (high-rise point block); Indicative density: 75 units per hectare; Diversity level: low.

account of a complex range of sometimes competing objectives, including the concern that sustainability can sometimes be used to justify so-called 'town cramming'.

There are no nationally accepted standards operating in England and Wales as to what constitutes 'sustainable density', but higher densities are generally considered to be more sustainable than lower ones, particularly near public transport hubs. The now defunct PPG3 (Housing) formerly defined high density as being 60 dwellings per hectare (net) and medium density as being 30 dwellings per hectare (net). In practice, what is considered to be 'high' is benchmarked against older suburban models of typically 15 to 20 units per hectare (net), which are now considered too low to be sustainable, compared with, say, the 100+ units per hectare achievable in mid-rise perimeter apartment blocks. Barton et al., for example, state that as a general principle 'the overall average density should be higher than the current suburban average', and they go on to suggest that 50 units per hectare (120 ppha) is a fair average density to aim for.[107] In city centre locations, where higher than average land prices occur, however, commensurately higher densities may be required to justify them. Campbell argues that the high density model has salved our conscience on sustainability but hasn't produced balanced communities.[108] He advocates that we now need to focus on medium-density typologies found in the best parts of many cities by instituting procedures for developing land in smaller parcels.

The National Planning Policy Framework now requires local planning authorities to set out their own approach to density to reflect local circumstances.[109] This would seem to be at odds with the government's overall drive to reduce confusion at the national level, which it attributes to there being too many standards in operation. However, it must also be read in conjunction with other policy strands, such as the policy requirement for developments *to be located and designed to minimise the number and length of car journeys and to maximise sustainable modes*: something that

can only be realistically achieved by promoting higher densities in close proximity to existing or planned facilities and services.

The notional examples of different block and plot configurations in this chapter approximate gross densities because they include the block as a unit and the different land uses within the block (where relevant) as well as the footpath and half the area of carriageway surrounding the block, but they do not include strategic public open space or other potential single-use developments, such as churches.

Notwithstanding this, and all other things being equal, it can be demonstrated that close-grain development of mixed-use street buildings combining active ground floors with apartments (flats and/or duplexes) overhead can (depending on apartment sizes) facilitate gross densities of over 100 dwellings per hectare (240+ ppha), comparable to densities of other mid-rise block types up to four or five storeys in height.

Townhouses can achieve the next highest density in the close-grain repertoire, with densities decreasing with wider plots and greater set-backs. In most cases, however, it is also demonstrably possible to achieve densities well in excess of the net density standard of 30 dwellings per hectare (70 ppha) minimum previously stipulated by PPG3 (cancelled) and the net density of 30 to 50 dwellings per hectare (70 to 120 ppha) for institutional and suburban lands stipulated in its Irish equivalent, the *Sustainable Residential Development Guidelines for Planning Authorities* (appropriate density ranges for inner suburban sites being set by the planning authority for inner suburban areas).

5.3   DETERMINING VIABILITY

It is something of a truism that neighbourhoods need facilities and services, and that facilities and services need neighbourhoods – that is, people. It should also go without saying that some facilities and services need more people

POPULATION CATCHMENTS FOR KEY SERVICES

Service	Indicative catchment population
Nursery school	2,000–4,000
Primary school	4,000+
Secondary school	8,000–16,000
Health centre (four doctors)	10,000–12,000
Local shop	1,500–5,000
Pub	5,000–7,000
Post office	5,000–10,000
Community centre	4,000–15,000
Library	12,000–30,000
District centre (superstore)	25,000–40,000
Leisure centre	25,000–40,000

Source: Adapted from the *Final Report of the Urban Task Force*[110] and Barton, H., Grant, M. and Guise, R.[111]

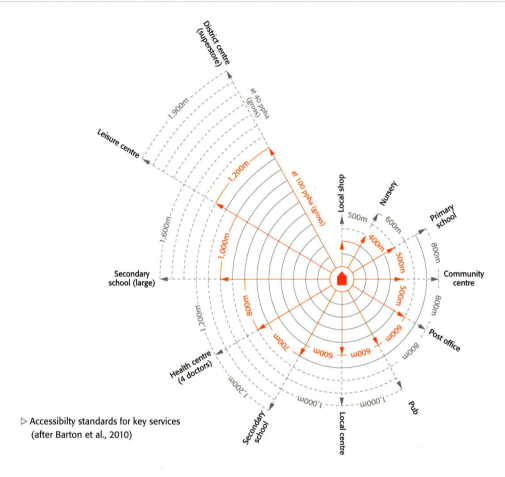

▷ Accessibilty standards for key services
(after Barton et al., 2010)

than others in order to make them viable. For example, a supermarket requires a much larger population to support it than, say, a pub or a local convenience shop.

Population thresholds required to support key facilities and services are provided in the *Urban Design Compendium 2,* Barton et al. and the report of the Urban Task Force.[112] However, as Barton et al. comprehensively demonstrate, achieving sufficient population densities within reasonable walking distances is a critical factor influencing whether the symbiotic nature of the relationship between the neighbourhood and its facilities and services can be made sustainable both in economic *and* transport terms.[113] Moreover, the distances people are prepared to walk to access different services varies, and also varies between neighbourhoods. For example, people are less prepared to walk to a supermarket than to a local pub. To complicate matters, the distance people actually have to walk within a given straight-line (as the crow flies) radius of the facility in question varies according to the unique topography of the place (for example, having to detour to cross a bridge can significantly extend the

route) and, more importantly for the purposes of this book, it also varies depending on the urban structure of the place, which is a critical factor making routes more or less direct.

Thus three key concepts in the provision and viability of local services are:

☐ density of population – expressed as persons per hectare (ppha)

☐ accessibility standards – the distance a certain proportion of people can be expected to walk

☐ urban structure and form – the directness of routes in so far as this affects both the catchment population and accessibility (in terms of accessibility; for example, Barton et al. assume that 'bendy routes' – i.e. non-direct routes – equate to 75% of the direct-line radius, representing about 55% of the theoretical catchment population).

Barton et al.'s calculations indicate that gross population density (including all the local land uses) is a surer indicator of catchment population than net density, and that 600 m is a reasonable accessibility standard to aim for in terms of most local facilities and services. At this distance Barton et al.'s research suggests that approximately 70% of trips will be non-motorised and, at a gross density of 60 ppha, a catchment of 6,000 people can be achieved: enough to nominally support a pub, a local shop, a local centre, a nursery school, a primary school, a community centre and a post office. At 60 ppha, they also suggest that 1,500 m is the best that can be achieved for an assumed catchment of 24,000 people: enough to support a district centre/superstore or a leisure centre, but at this distance the percentage of people prepared to walk drops dramatically.

The implication is that new housing should be located within 600 m of an existing or planned neighbourhood centre (assuming a residential density of not less than 60 ppha) or within 1,500 m of a district-level service, such as a superstore or a secondary school. Between these two figures, the oft-quoted 'pedshed' of 800 m is a good starting point, equating to approximately 60% of trips on foot.

Barton et al. go on to point out, however, that people may well choose not to use their local services (for example, they may choose to use a dentist or a doctor that is outside their local area) and that viability will be bolstered by grouping facilities and services together in the most visible locations that are also accessible to public transport and passing traffic. Grouping of facilities and services together helps mutually supporting uses, and increases consumer choice and the likelihood of people making linked trips.

5.4   MIXING COMPATIBLE USES

Different uses can be mixed vertically or horizontally. Vertical mixed uses occur within the same building: for example, apartments over shops. Horizontal mixed uses occur side by side: for example, apartments next to shops. The traditional street building typology is characterised by vertical mixed uses; however, as described in Chapter 4, there are significant challenges to replicating this in new developments.

In broad terms most small-scale uses can be mixed vertically and/or horizontally in street buildings. This includes apartments and duplexes, small shops, pubs, restaurants, cafés, banks, post offices, professional services (solicitors, accountants, architects, doctors, dentists, etc.), hairdressers, beauty salons and their like. More land-hungry uses, such as schools, on the other hand, usually require a different setting.

Similarly, while uses such as professional services can operate successfully above ground level, others, like most shops, rely on passing trade, and so require more visible locations as well as a high rate of footfall.

Active ground-floor uses (such as shops, restaurants or cafés) are preferable from an urban design and planning point of view, because these have the potential to activate the public realm, with residential and/or office uses overhead. However, while some uses positively complement each other (e.g. offices and cafés), others (e.g. apartments and pubs) can be incompatible. Although mixing of residential uses with pubs and restaurants and their like can cause problems, many of the issues, such as smell and noise nuisance caused by air handling and ventilation outlets, can be designed out (see Chapter 6) and, for some people, the perceived benefits may outweigh the disadvantages.

Although it is highly desirable to accommodate retail, commercial *and* residential uses vertically, it is not usually possible to incorporate more than one access to the upper floors from the street. This means that any and all upper-floor uses will typically have to share an entrance and vertical circulation space. Although commercial and residential uses typically alternate between being occupied predominantly

△ Close-grain (mixed-use) street, Tübingen, Germany

during the day and during the night respectively, this can raise maintenance and security issues and makes it more difficult to comply with Building Regulations.

Consequently, in addition to overall viability, it is necessary to consider:

☐ the setting for the use (e.g. visibility and footfall)

☐ the floor space required (e.g. can the use be accommodated on a single floor level?)

☐ patterns of usage (daytime versus night-time)

☐ whether uses are complementary/symbiotic (e.g. offices and cafés)

☐ traffic generation

☐ whether there are potential conflicts (e.g. noise and/or smell nuisance).

Where it can be anticipated that commercial uses will not be viable in the short to medium term, it may be appropriate to provide for residential ground-floor uses in the interim while designing in adaptability for changes of use later. Typically this will require higher ground-floor-to-ceiling heights, and use of cross-wall construction to avoid placing of structural members within the available space, thereby maximising future changes internally without the use of loadbearing partitions.

In the case of Vauban, there was little take-up of close-grain plots for mixed uses by building cooperative groups. As a result, commercial ground-floor uses are located in medium-grain blocks with apartments overhead, focused on the main spine of the neighbourhood, with close-grain townhouses located on secondary streets running perpendicular to this spine. In contrast, the masterplan for Tübingen Südstadt required building cooperatives to come with proposals for mixed-use ground floors.

5.5 CONFIGURING THE BLOCK AND PLOT

The advantages of the perimeter block typology over other types is outlined in Chapter 2. The perimeter block typology is inherently flexible and can combine a range of plot sizes and building types in many different configurations and densities.

It facilitates a clear distinction between the public and private domain, with building 'fronts' overlooking the street, and inactive 'backs' oriented towards the rear. The distinction between 'fronts' and 'backs' fosters an active yet safe urban environment and contributes to legibility by signalling the transition between what is public and what is private. It allows the privacy and security of shared and private open spaces to be maintained, and access, parking and general activity associated with the front of buildings to be focused on the street. The perimeter block also maintains continuity of the building line, and provides a sense of enclosure to the street.

Private and semi-private open space can be provided in the interior of the block together with access for services and, if necessary, additional parking. For these reasons, the perimeter block typology is advocated as being the most suited to designing for diversity, at least in a European context.

The configuration of the perimeter block in its many and varied permutations requires careful consideration.

5.5.1 Block size and shape

'Close-' (or 'fine-') grain streets tend to have smaller block sizes and relatively dense patterns of plot subdivision, compared with medium- or 'coarse-' grain ones.

Smaller blocks generate a more flexible grid and permit more frequent linkages, visual and pedestrian connectivity, and a greater degree of activity on the street; however, small blocks provide lower potential for mixed uses or mixed plot sizes, lower overall densities, reduced potential for biodiversity and reduced area for potential development, and entail higher costs of infrastructural provision.

Block sizes ranging from 50 m to 100 m provide a good rule of thumb, with sizes between 60 m and 80 m striking a good balance between these competing demands.

Square blocks are generally versatile; however, rectangular blocks are better able to accommodate the larger footprints needed for commercial uses. Rectangular blocks may also be adapted to sloping ground, with the long side of the block following contour lines more readily. Rectangular blocks with the short side fronting the main street can also facilitate greater penetration of the surroundings because they present less continuous frontage to the main street. The same principles apply to distorted grids or irregularly shaped blocks that respond to pre-existing urban morphologies, topography or the whims of the designer. Cranked or distorted grids can add interest and variety as well as helping to slow traffic. The side effect of creating distorted plot shapes within the block is that it can result in awkward building forms and/or juxtaposition of buildings and less usable curtilage.

5.5.2 Plot size and configuration

Historically, plot sizes have been determined by the development market. The density and intensity of plot subdivisions generated by past urban conditions, however, is not desirable now. Although there is no minimum plot size, the benefits of achieving close-grain development need to be reconciled with standards and expectations that influence the sizes of dwellings and open space etc., and must be tempered by the need to achieve an economically viable mix of uses, forms and tenures overall.

△ CAD rendering of Keret House,
   (Jakub Szczesny)

▷ 3D model of Keret House
   (Jakub Szczesny)

This proposal for a writer's studio on a 1.33 m wide site in Warsaw, Poland, by Jakub Szczesny illustrates what is possible on even the narrowest of sites. The project is concerned with inserting an alien intellectual presence to observe the city's cultural situation and to create a platform for intellectual exchange, not with 'narrowness' *per se*, but it does have a residential programme. While it will occupy a 'left over' gap between buildings, and not an intentional building plot, it is noteworthy that the studio doesn't comply with Polish building regulations and so consent was sought as an art installation.

While there are no standards for plot size in the UK or Ireland, there are a plethora of standards affecting dwelling size, private and public open space and room sizes that indirectly affect plot size, particularly within blocks. To complicate matters:

☐ there is little consistency between standards

☐ their status and applicability vary

☐ some standards are contradictory in their effect

☐ there is considerable overlap between them.

Further, the political appetite for imposing standards at the national level, which have in the past been applied to both public sector and publicly subsidised developments, waxes and wanes according to the leanings of different political administrations. At the same time, individual local authorities frequently apply their own unique standards, and these are subject to ongoing review and change.

In addition to the Building Regulations, the most influential standards operating at the national level include the following:

Code for Sustainable Homes, updated in 2010 (Department for Communities and Local Government). The Code for Sustainable Homes sets national standards for the sustainable design and construction of new homes. It applies in England, Wales and Northern Ireland. The Code uses a system of credits and mandatory requirements to measure sustainability against nine categories, and generates a star rating indicating the overall performance of the dwelling of between 1 and 6 (6 being the highest). Of particular relevance to the design of building plots is that detailed specification for storage of both non-recyclable and recyclable waste is a mandatory requirement required to achieve any rating. Credits are also allocated for cycle storage and space for home working. Since it came into operation in 2007, local authority-funded housing in England, Wales and Northern Ireland has been required to meet Code level 3.[114] This will rise to level 4 in the next HCA funding programme.

Housing Quality Indicators (HQIs), revised in 2008 (Homes and Communities Agency). HQIs are a measurement and assessment tool that intends to evaluate housing schemes on the basis of quality rather than just cost. They incorporate the design standards required of affordable housing providers receiving funding through the National Affordable Housing Programme (NAHP) and Affordable Homes Programme (AHP). The indicators are location, site (visual impact, layout and landscaping, open space, routes and movement), unit size and layout, noise, light, services and adaptability, accessibility, sustainability and the external environment (Building for Life – see Chapter 3). HQIs also encompass aspects of Secured by Design, Standards and Quality in Housing Association Development and the Code for Sustainable Homes.

Lifetime Homes, updated 2010 (Habinteg Housing Association and the Joseph Rowntree Foundation). The core aim of these 16 design criteria is to make dwellings accessible and adaptable to the changing needs of their inhabitants, particularly in old age. In practice, this involves increasing space provision for circulation and bathrooms, which is broadly accepted by housing associations producing housing for rent but tends to be resisted by developers, because it can result in an over proliferation of bathrooms at the expense of habitable space. Local authorities commonly require compliance but, as Levitt points out, the standards are difficult to meet in narrow-fronted houses and three-storey houses (because domestic chair lifts are designed to rise through two storeys).[115] Achieving the Code for Sustainable Homes level 6 requires full compliance with Lifetime Homes. Since 2011, all public sector-funded housing in England, Wales and Northern Ireland is expected to be built to the Lifetime Homes standard, with a target of 2013 for all private sector dwellings.

Secured by Design, established 1989 (Association of Chief Police Officers in England and Wales). This is the corporate title of a police initiative supported by the government. Secured by Design criteria are summarised in *Safer Places: The Planning System and Crime Prevention*.[116] Their aim is to reduce crime by designing buildings and spaces that reduce opportunities for criminals. The document discourages intrusion into schemes by non-residents as well as laneway access to the back of plots. The implications of this, as discussed in more detail below, are contentious from an urban design point of view, particularly in regard to mixed-use developments, where it is a specific objective to attract non-residents. Many local authorities require that new developments meet Secured by Design criteria.

London Housing Design Guide, 2010 interim edition (London Development Agency). This document is primarily focused on internal space standards. These standards are applied to HCA-funded projects and projects of all tenures on HCA lands (in London). Although limited in geographical spread to London, this document is of interest because it encompasses the key elements of the Code for Sustainable Homes, Housing Quality Indicators, Secured by Design and Lifetime Homes standards.[117] The London Plan, 2011, sets minimum space standards for all new residential development and states the intention to produce Supplementary Planning Guidance (SPG) for housing that will draw on this design guide.[118]

Standards and Quality in Housing Association Development, updated in 2008 (National Housing Federation). The NHF represents Housing Associations in England. Accordingly, these standards are aimed at affordable housing. They avoid political resistance to quantitative space requirements by focusing on the space and furniture layouts needed to accommodate essential domestic activities. These are incorporated in the HCA's Housing Quality Indicators.

Sustainable Urban Housing Design Standards for New Apartments: Guidelines for Planning Authorities, 2007 (Department of the Environment, Heritage and Local Government of Ireland (now the Department of the Environment, Communities and Local Government)). Although these standards are guidelines, Irish planning authorities are required to have regard to them. This confers on them a quasi-statutory status. The guidelines set out minimum sizes for apartments as well as minimum sizes for balconies, minimum room sizes and minimum floor-to-ceiling heights (3 m for ground floors and 2.7 m for upper floors); however, they urge planning authorities to set target averages that require a proportion of units to exceed the mimima.

An informative summary of space standards is provided by Levitt[119]; however, it is fruitless to try to suggest a universally applicable set of standards, not least because expectations change. That said, the following should be borne in mind:

Plot width

In England and Wales, Parts B and E of the Building Regulations set out, respectively, requirements for fire separation and acoustic separation that by influencing the construction and thickness of party walls have a slight yet significant effect on the width of frontages for contiguous buildings (see Chapter 6 for further information).

Part M1 requires reasonable provision for people to gain access to and use the building and its facilities. The Approved Document accompanying Part M (ADM) indicates a fairly prescriptive means of satisfying the Regulations, drawing heavily on BS 8300:2001 'Design of Buildings and their approaches to meet the needs of disabled people – Code of Practice' (updated 2009). However, it acknowledges that there may be other equally satisfactory ways of meeting the requirements. ADM advises that any proposed alternatives should be accompanied by an Access Statement, in order to assist the Building Control Authority in reaching a decision as to whether reasonable provision has been made.

ADM sets out detailed guidance relating to corridor widths, door openings and sizes of wheelchair-accessible WCs that have significant implications for the width and location of visitable WCs, that in turn have knock-on effects on building footprints and, consequently, on plot widths.

Lifetime Homes standards (Joseph Rowntree Foundation) amplify access requirements, including increased space at the leading edge of doors, space for showers in accessible WCs and additional width of stairs for stair-lifts. The Homes and Community Agency's Design and Quality Standards have implications broadly similar to the Building Regulations and Lifetime Homes, but with wider requirements for door openings and a presumption against stair winders. These all have space implications for dwelling footprints that, because they are increasingly sought by local authorities as evidence of design quality and/or as prerequisites for funding support, are consequently influential in planning terms.

The combined effect of these requirements is that very narrow plots (less than, say, 4 m) can only be achieved where circulation is not separated from habitable rooms. This, in turn, makes narrower plots less adaptable to larger families, and effectively restricts dwelling height to two storeys.

Plot width is also influenced by the need to span between party walls economically, affecting the balance of costs and benefits arising from the greater flexibility of wider plots against their reduced densities. The commonly available depth of 220 mm solid timber sections, for example, provides a versatile joist size capable of spanning up to about 5.5 m between party walls (depending on width, spacing and load).[120]

For mixed-use street buildings, sufficient plot width is required to accommodate viable small-unit retail or commercial frontage at ground level, with separate access and space for vertical circulation, space requirements for a range of dual-aspect mixed uses above and provision of private open space and servicing. The *Urban Design Compendium* recommends that buildings of between 5 m and 7 m wide provide extremely flexible cells, but notes that below 5.5 m it is difficult to extend backwards without unduly reducing available light and ventilation. Although there is some flexibility in plot depth, a rule of thumb indicates a minimum practical width of 6 m for mixed-use buildings, assuming that a passenger lift is not provided. On this basis, an average width of between 6 m and 10 m is a reasonable expectation. Up to about 15 m may be required for corner plots to allow flexibility in space-planning where the block turns the corner (returns) at the junction of two streets.

Plot gradient

The buildability of sloping plots is significantly affected by Part M of the Building Regulations. In particular, guidance contained in the Approved Document accompanying Part M (ADM) has the effect of discouraging stepped access to buildings. The objective of this part of the guidance is to provide a suitable means of access from the boundary of the plot and from any car-parking that is provided on plot to the building, by minimising the difference in height between the entrance storey and the point of entry to the site.

This discourages raising internal floor levels above natural ground level, which in turn reduces potential to mitigate the perceived loss of security and privacy in townhouses, especially those having reduced (or no) front set-back from the street. This is of particular relevance to the revival of townhouses as a typology in more urban or peri-urban locations, where urban design objectives to limit front set-backs (for example, to raise density and provide a satisfactory sense of enclosure to the street) and to avoid on-plot car-parking, do not harmonise with the preference of house buyers, particularly those with families, for deeper front set-backs.

ADM defines plot gradient as the gradient measured between the finished floor of the dwelling and the point of access. A plot gradient of more than 1:15 is considered to be steeply sloping. The approach should be to provide for an approach to the principal entrance that is as level as possible; failing that, to an alternative entrance. Where gradients are greater than 1:15 owing to topographical constraints, however, a stepped approach may be considered reasonable.

To overcome this, it may be possible to incorporate raised internal floor levels subject to satisfying access requirements within the interior of the block, where more space can be made available to provide ramped access. As noted above, ADM suggests that any proposed alternatives should be accompanied by an Access Statement in order to assist the Building Control Authority in reaching a decision as to whether reasonable provision has been made. Clearly, such an approach (which is favoured in the Netherlands) would also need to be investigated in advance of seeking planning permission in order avoid the potential for costly delay at later stages.

Plot depth

One of the most contentious yet influential 'standards', which appears in many local authority requirements but not in national ones, is the separation distance between opposing rear windows. A separation distance of 22 m is commonly sought, imposing a minimum depth of rear garden (for back-to-back plots) of 11 m. Some local authorities increase the distance over sloping ground. The *Urban Design Compendium* suggests that a separation distance of 20 m is a good rule of thumb, with reduced distances suitable for mews developments. Reduced distances are also commonly accepted where back windows face gables, or where windows are not directly opposing.

The 22 m 'rule' is a legacy of the Tudor Walters Report on housing for the working classes published in 1918, in the wake of World War I, which subsequently found its way into development control standards. The standard emerged from the report's recommendation to provide a distance of 70 feet separation between facing windows of houses, on the basis that this would ensure adequate sunlight to dwellings (specifically one hour of sunlight to a ground south-facing window in London on the shortest day of the year). Cowan's *Dictionary of Urbanism* wryly points out that the alternative belief, that 22 m was chosen as being the shortest distance at which it was considered impossible to see a nipple, is erroneous.[121] Nevertheless this was transmuted over the decades into a standard intended to provide adequate privacy between the facing windows of dwellings.

It remains a truism that while urban dwellers may have reduced expectations of privacy compared to suburban ones, this reflects socio-economic factors more than the need for privacy *per se*. It can also be pointed out that designing dwellings to achieve total privacy is counterproductive because this can contribute to social isolation and vulnerability to crime. There is clearly some scope for empirical research in this area; however, this would certainly encounter difficulties. For example, how can expectations of privacy be measured empirically, much less standardised across a plethora of different socio-cultural conditions and expectations? Suffice to say that solar access remains a function of purely physical factors, whether or not standards for sunlight (and/or daylight) are imposed. Further discussion on sunlight and daylight considerations is provided in Chapter 6. In any case, the 22 m separation distance seems to be accepted by both house buyers and by planners alike, and, ultimately, 'what matters is what works'.

Although there are numerous cases where buildings with less deep plots can be shown to achieve a satisfactory amount of private open space as well as adequate privacy, these invariably involve single-aspect dwellings and/or design-specific approaches to the arrangement of rooms and orientation of window openings and the like.

Relying on a design solution to resolve potential privacy conflicts, however, requires the overall design of the development as a whole to be determined by a single designer or by close collaboration between different designers. Where blocks are allocated to different designers on a block-by-block basis, this can facilitate shallower plots and, consequently, can result in a degree of difference between blocks. This defeats the purpose of designing blocks and plot subdivisions within which different designers, self builders, cooperative building groups or small-scale developers can operate within the same block with minimal coordination and, preferably, minimal planning control.

The *Urban Design Compendium* suggests a rule of thumb for 20 m deep plots in the case of townhouses. To achieve a rear set-back of 11 m, however, leaves a challenging 9 m within which to accommodate both the building envelope and any front set-back. A set-back of between 1.5 m and 2 m is needed to provide the sense of security for habitable rooms demanded by the market (preferably in conjunction with a change in level), yet be small enough to prevent front gardens from being lost to on-plot car-parking at a later date.

The illustrated example of close-grain plots in Steigereiland, Ijburg, set out plots of 6 m wide by 22 m deep, and stipulated a building envelope comprising a maximum building footprint of 12 m deep, and a maximum height of 13.5 m with no front set-back. In the event, all the houses were built to the maximum allowed depth, resulting in rear set-back of 10 m (equivalent to 20 m between opposing windows for equivalent back-to-back plots). The absence of a front set-back perhaps illustrates a greater acceptance of higher-density living and a willingness to experiment on the part of the Dutch but, as in the example shown by ANA Architects, this is mitigated by the incorporation of a live-work space in the ground floor front room, which forms an effective buffer space between the street and domestic living spaces.

The UK police initiative supporting the principles of 'designing out crime', *Secured by Design*, discourages plots with rear access.[122] This has significant implications for achieving separation distances between opposing windows and provision for gaining access to rear gardens from the street.

△▷ Townhouse with live-work unit at ground level, Steigereiland, Ijburg, the Netherlands (ANA Architects)

section A

1 entrance hall
2 workspace
3 kitchen
4 terrace
5 living
6 hobby
7 hall
8 bedroom
9 walk in closet
10 bathroom
11 guest room
12 storage
13 laundry

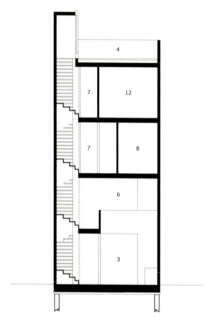

section B

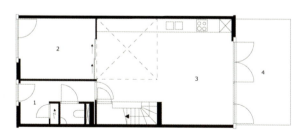

ground floor

Back-to-back gardens also reduce the potential for future subdivision to provide mews development and live-work opportunities that, by activating rear lanes, would have the combined benefit of facilitating increased densities, greater diversity and access to rear gardens without creating unsupervised laneways. The incorporation of a rear access laneway can also serve to reduce plot depths necessary to achieve a given separation distance, so that these benefits can be achieved without sacrificing density. Front set-backs are indirectly affected by the Code for Sustainable Homes standards, which set out requirements for recycling bins, bicycle storage and access to meters, with consequent knock-on effects on overall plot depths. Detailed design considerations affecting the interface between plots and the public realm are considered more fully in Chapter 6.

For mixed-use street buildings, sufficient plot depth is required to accommodate viable small-unit retail or commercial floor plates at ground level, and space requirements for a range of dual-aspect mixed uses above. Although there is some flexibility in plot depth, a rule of thumb indicates a range between 20 m and 40 m (where mews-type accommodation at the rear is also provided). Provision of basement accommodation ancillary to the ground floor provides added flexibility.

5.5.3 Corners

Corner sites have two frontages and are visually prominent. The potential this confers on them for more entrances to the building makes them especially suited to mixed uses. The dilemma for close-grain corner buildings (and their plots), however, is how can a two-dimensional type – expressed as a space between two party walls – turn a corner to address two streets simultaneously?

Conventional close-grain development – open and closed row housing – is usually characterised by repetition. By its nature, this form of development shuns diversity, with repetition frequently carried to its logical conclusion by terminating the ends of rows with units that are identical to their neighbours. This typically results in a blank gable facing the secondary street frontage, resulting in reduced surveillance, and presents a blank canvas to would-be graffiti artists.

Historically, Georgian townhouses took two contrasting approaches to corners. Where they met a street of secondary significance, such as a mews or access lane, they either ignored it or provided a composition of blind windows (or in some cases, an oriel window). Where the status of both streets was deemed to be equal, however, a common approach was to squeeze two square-shaped units, each one room deep with a staircase in opposite corners, often with no yard or windows to the rear. In this way, as McCullogh describes, 'They take full part in the scenographic character of the city – celebrating corners with niches and elegant doorways, but it is a wafer thin urbanity, an agreed untruth.'[123]

Single-aspect units are still commonly used to resolve corners of apartment blocks, whereas modern row housing often continues to ignore the issue or to provide wider corner plots without changing the house type to respond to the secondary street. The commonplace approach adopted in many older suburban housing developments of dividing corner plots diagonally, for occupation by a pair of semi-detached units, creates a chamfer to the building line that doesn't properly address the corner, and creates awkward triangular-shaped gardens.

None of these approaches can be said to be entirely satisfactory. The design of plots needs to respond to this while the rules for their development also need to be articulated to ensure that the resulting plan layout achieves a satisfactory compromise between the need to address the street and avoiding unduly contorted space-planning.

The most satisfactory compromise is to ensure that internal space-planning properly addresses both aspects to the street. In the case of townhouses, where a front set back is desirable for security and privacy, space-planning may be

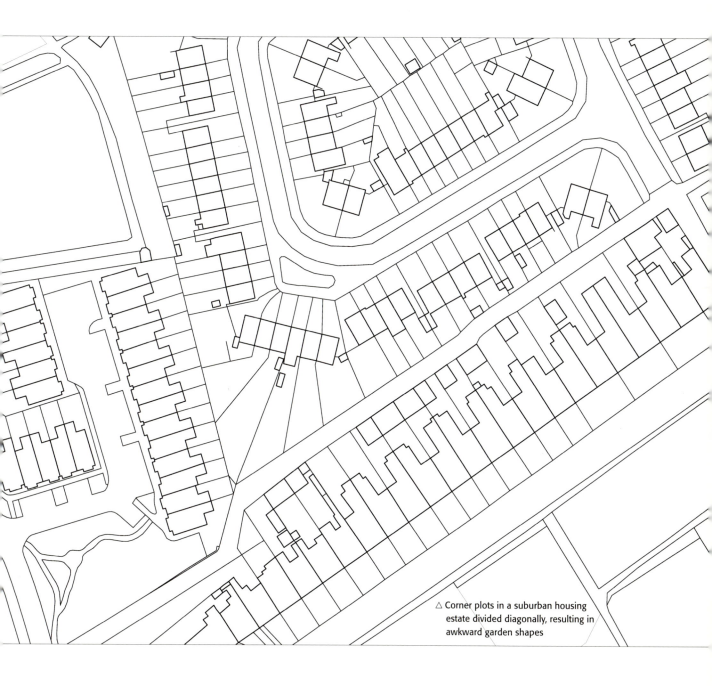

△ Corner plots in a suburban housing
estate divided diagonally, resulting in
awkward garden shapes

eased by a wider corner plot. A reduced plot depth may be used to reduce the overall increase in plot area compared to mid-row plots, because the rear windows of corner units will not directly oppose their nearest neighbours. A wider corner plot may also be required for mixed-use plots in order to provide dual-aspect upper floors that don't give rise to undue levels of overbearing or overlooking of neighbouring plots.

5.5.4 Grain

Experience shows that long narrow (oblong) plots are preferable because they maximise the number of plots that can share frontage to any given length of street. Narrow plots facilitate efficient building forms and maximise activity, diversity and interest on the street.

For mixed-use street buildings no minimum width of frontage should be required in principle; however, the balance of floor space, daylighting, open space and vertical circulation requirements makes plot widths less than 6 m difficult to achieve.

In the case of townhouses, reduced plot widths are more feasible, but ultimately the same constraints apply to make widths of less than 5 m challenging to designers.

Despite the technical difficulties of meeting space standards and building regulations associated with very narrow plots, the approach of not stipulating minimum plot widths was adopted in Tübingen Südstadt, to facilitate participation by people from a broader socio-economic spectrum, allowing their architects to come up with innovative solutions to those challenges. It is noteworthy, however, that in the case of Tübingen proposals were required to be advanced by building cooperative groups rather than individual plots being released to the open market, making it easier for building on narrower plots to be coordinated as part of an overall subdivision plan for the block.

5.6 A TOOLKIT FOR DESIGNING CLOSE- AND MIXED-GRAIN BLOCKS AND PLOTS

The following section is a toolkit comprising a series of diagrams together with a table of indicative block and plot sizes. The diagrams indicate some of the principal strategic block and plot options available to the masterplanner, each with varying potential for combining a mix of uses, live-work, architectural variety, mixed typologies and mix of plot sizes. The data is summarised in tabular form as a 'ready reckoner' that can be used by the masterplanner to help determine the appropriate size and configuration of blocks and plots and, at subsequent stages, to test their feasibility.

The strategic design options illustrated are:

☐ close-grain (mainly residential) perimeter block with back-to-back plots

☐ close-grain (mainly residential) perimeter block with shared parking court

☐ close-grain (mainly residential) perimeter block with rear access lane

☐ close-grain (mainly residential) perimeter block with shared courtyard

☐ close-grain (mainly residential) perimeter block with shared courtyard and parking court

☐ close-grain (mainly residential) perimeter block with double-loaded access

☐ close-grain (mixed-use) hybrid block with through plots

☐ mixed-grain (mixed-use) perimeter block with rear access lane

☐ medium-grain (mainly residential) perimeter block with shared courtyard

- □ close-grain (mixed-use) perimeter block with shared podium courtyard

- □ medium-grain (mixed-use) perimeter block.

All of the block diagrams are variants of the perimeter block typology, and they all encapsulate the same basic strategic design principles:

- □ ensure fronts of buildings face fronts and backs face backs

- □ maximise the number of entrances on the street

- □ focus car-parking on the street (coordinate with plot subdivision as much as possible to facilitate overlooking of communal spaces)

- □ minimise turning radii to slow traffic and avoid pedestrian pinch points at corner plots

- □ size blocks having regard to plot subdivision to optimise density, taking account of the interrelationship between front set-backs, likely building footprints and back-to-back/private open space requirements

- □ ensure the width of corner plots can facilitate building frontages turning corners and potential for future changes of use (e.g. corner shops).

For simplicity, all of the diagrams are intended to be non-place specific, and so are drawn as simple orthogonal shapes. In reality, the size and shape of blocks would be influenced by a range of contextual factors such as topography, existing features and orientation. They are not exhaustive; nor can they be, because the scope for variety is immense.

The accompanying plot diagrams draw on 'generic' plans to illustrate the interrelationship between block size and shape, plot width, plot depth, building footprint and density, assuming a minimum front set-back for residential ground floors of

2 m and a minimum back-to-back separation distance for residential upper floors of 22 m (reduced for mews). The building plans[124] are indicated solely for the purpose of illustrating the relationship between building size and plot size, and are not intended to advocate 'ideal' plans. These plot sizes provide a robust starting point for the design of blocks capable of accommodating a given degree of diversity, without relying on special design solutions. However, the amount of coordination that will be required in practice will be influenced by a number of contributory factors, such as whether plots are required to be capable of being developed on an ad hoc basis, in groups or in one go, as well as the intended mix of uses, and adaptability to change.

The guidance focuses on robust building typologies that have stood the test of time: the mixed-use street building, townhouse, mansion block (terraced apartments) and the apartment block. It avoids recent typologies such as deck-access flats and stacked maisonettes for three reasons. First, they are problematic in terms of access, privacy and security, requiring special design solutions to overcome these issues. Second, they do not lend themselves to mixed uses or changes of use. Third, they tend to be resisted by the development market. As a result, they are of limited applicability to plot-based approaches to masterplanning.

5.6.1 Close-grain

(mainly residential) perimeter block with back-to-back plots

This is one of the simplest and most common perimeter block types. The block is composed of oblong-shaped plots with the short side of each plot facing the street. Each plot shares a boundary with a neighbouring plot at its rear and side or sides.

The depth of the block on one axis is effectively determined by the depth of the plots, which may themselves vary in width and/or depth. The length of the block on its second axis is limited only by the number of plots laid side by side; however, in practice this is limited by the need to create a permeable and walkable street network.

The ends of blocks may be terminated by back-to-back plots with the long side of the plot facing the street; however, this typically results in the gable ends of buildings facing the street. For this reason, it is preferable for plots to turn the corner so that the street is overlooked on each side of the block.

Because these end plots are not directly opposed to the plots behind them, the distance between directly opposing windows is increased. This can allow less deep plots to be considered at the ends of the block, subject to the need to provide sufficient space at the rear and sunlight. Reducing plot depths at the ends of the block also needs to be reconciled with potential for 'oblique' overlooking.

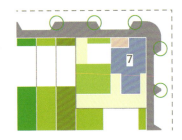

△ Close-grain residential block with back-to-back plots

0   10m   20m

1. Back-to-back plots
2. End plots turned 90° from back-to-back plots
3. Potential for extension and/or change of use of corner buildings
4. Oblique overlooking
5. On-street parking
6. Corner plot designed with equivalent set-back to overlook both frontages
7. Corner plots amalgamated to provide mixed-use buildings
8. Lower ground floor with potential for live-work (overleaf)

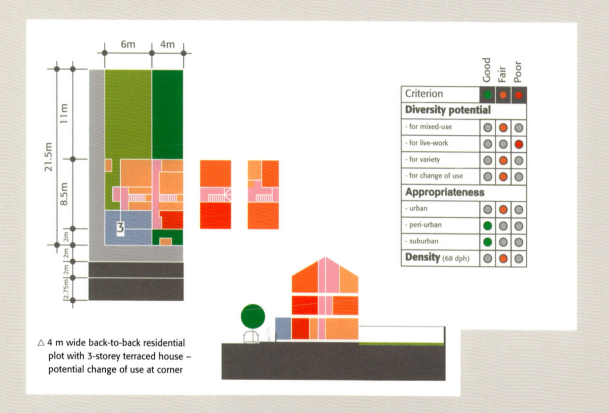

	Good	Fair	Poor
Criterion	🟢	🔴	🔴
Diversity potential			
- for mixed-use	⚪	⚪	⚪
- for live-work	⚪	⚪	🔴
- for variety	⚪	🔴	⚪
- for change of use	⚪	🔴	⚪
Appropriateness			
- urban	⚪	🔴	⚪
- peri-urban	🟢	⚪	⚪
- suburban	🟢	⚪	⚪
Density (68 dph)	⚪	🔴	⚪

△ 4 m wide back-to-back residential plot with 3-storey terraced house – potential change of use at corner

The shape of the block and the shape of its constituent plots are interdependent. Rectangular blocks and plots facilitate the most efficient arrangement, but the need to respond to topography and other factors often results in 'deformed grids' with irregularly shaped blocks. The more irregular the plots shapes, however, the greater the knock-on effect on the space-planning of buildings, particularly if the width of plots requires buildings to share plot boundaries.

Limiting the front set-back on narrow plots as indicated in the example shown also means that parking to serve mid-row plots must be accommodated on the street. Corner plots are more flexible in terms of their potential to accommodate parking on plot because they have two frontages.

The depth of back-to-back housing plots is influenced by the need to provide adequate private open space, sunlight and privacy between opposing windows. The width of plots is determined by the need to provide adequate room sizes internally and other standards. Narrower plots in general permit higher densities to be achieved; however, housing plots of 4–5 m wide are generally limited to contiguous

(i.e. attached) buildings. The illustrated examples show the interrelationship between plot width and building footprint for two 4 m wide plots, based on generic housing layouts, assuming a front set-back of 2 m, and a separation distance of 22 m between opposing windows of back-to-back plots (i.e. 11 m each).

Given a typical minimum building depth of 8.5 m, this results in a plot depth of 21.5 m, and a gross density of around 68 dwellings per hectare. Corner plots are typically wider than mid-row plots in order to allow a building set-back from both frontages that also addresses the street on both sides. A tried and tested way of achieving this is by entering the building from the long side of the plot into the middle of the plan, which allows the full width of the plan at the front and rear to be given over to habitable rooms.

Corner plots also lend themselves to partial change of use to provide small-scale neighbourhood services, such as a corner shop. Alternatively, larger plots can be provided at corners in order to accommodate apartments or mixed-use commercial and apartment buildings.

The second example shows a similar plan arrangement but including a lower ground floor. This type lends itself to live-work practices, because the lower ground level can be accessed separately from the street. The potential for raising the upper ground-floor level above street level also makes it more private and thus more attractive; however, visitable access for the disabled must then be ramped or accessed from the rear, potentially requiring laneway or courtyard access to be introduced to the block. Imrie[125] cites examples of townhouse developments in the UK where access to the rear has been provided at grade, so that they can be made 'liveable' to people with disabilities rather than merely 'visitable' ■

△ Close-grain attached townhouses in Vauban, Freiburg, Germany

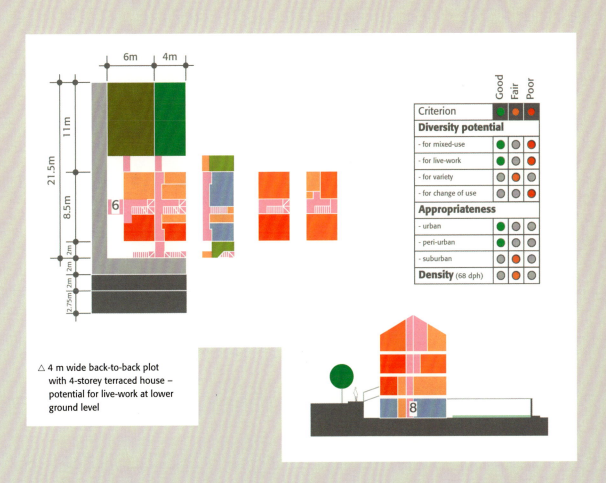

Criterion	Good	Fair	Poor
Diversity potential			
- for mixed-use	🟢	⚪	🔴
- for live-work	🟢	⚪	🔴
- for variety	⚪	🟠	⚪
- for change of use	⚪	⚪	🔴
Appropriateness			
- urban	🟢	⚪	⚪
- peri-urban	🟢	⚪	⚪
- suburban	⚪	🟠	⚪
Density (68 dph)	⚪	🟠	⚪

△ 4 m wide back-to-back plot with 4-storey terraced house – potential for live-work at lower ground level

5.6.2 Close-grain

(mainly residential) perimeter block with shared parking court

1. Parking court(s)
2. Live-work unit(s) overlook parking courts
3. Houses overlook parking courts
4. Wide plots can accommodate on-plot parking and/or different dwelling types
5. Plots configured to allow dual front and rear access
6. On-street parking
7. Corner plot(s) amalgamated to provide mixed-use buildings

0   10m   20m

△ Close-grain residential block with parking court overlooked by a combination of houses and live-work units with potential for commercial uses on corner plot(s)

This is a variation of the back-to-back plot arrangement, where part of the interior of the block is given over to parking. In simple terms, the plots no longer back on to one another but onto what is effectively shared space that (if not gated) is also accessible to the public. This has a number of implications both for the success of the courtyard space and for the arrangement and size of plots.

First and foremost, in order for these types of spaces to remain secure and well cared-for, they also need to be over-looked. Parking courts in Poundbury (masterplanned by Leon Krier) address this by 'chequer-boarding' plots, where one or more houses is placed at the rear of the plot over-looking the court rather than at the front facing onto the street. This results in the rear gardens of some plots facing the street and potential conflict between neighbouring build-ings that are out of alignment.

An alternative approach that lends itself particularly well to this type of block is to incorporate live-work elements facing the court. In the example shown, live-work units are also supplemented by plots directly facing the court that avoid backing onto the street.

A second implication is that plots are accessed from the parking court on a day-to-day basis as well as from the street, thereby diluting activity on the street.

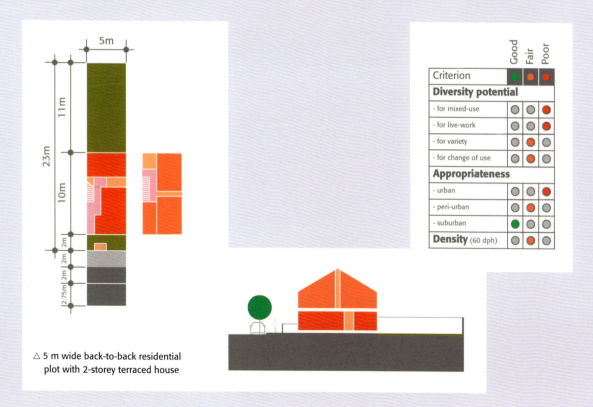

△ 5 m wide back-to-back residential
plot with 2-storey terraced house

Criterion	Good	Fair	Poor
Diversity potential			
- for mixed-use	○	○	●
- for live-work	○	○	●
- for variety	○	●	○
- for change of use	○	●	○
Appropriateness			
- urban	○	○	●
- peri-urban	○	●	○
- suburban	●	○	○
Density (60 dph)	○	●	○

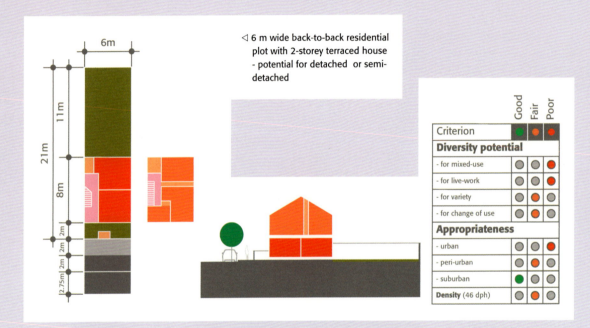

◁ 6 m wide back-to-back residential plot with 2-storey terraced house - potential for detached or semi-detached

Criterion	Good	Fair	Poor
Diversity potential			
- for mixed-use	○	○	●
- for live-work	○	○	●
- for variety	○	●	○
- for change of use	○	●	○
Appropriateness			
- urban	○	○	●
- peri-urban	○	●	○
- suburban	●	○	○
Density (46 dph)	○	●	○

Third, the introduction of the parking court adds distance between opposing windows, producing a greater separation distance between buildings using less deep plots. This results in a trade-off between plot depth and the lowering of density that results from increasing the overall size of the block.

In the example shown, wider plots are incorporated to compensate for space lost to the parking court. This facilitates greater flexibility in building footprints as well as the potential for on-plot parking behind the building line to supplement shared parking at the rear.

As in the case of the previous example, corner plots may be amalgamated to facilitate mixed-use buildings and/or flats.

The two plots illustrated show the effect of widening the plot to 5 m and 6 m respectively on the depth of the building footprint required to accommodate two generic (two-storey) row-house plans, and the knock-on effect this has on plot size and density. Assuming a fixed front set-back of 2 m and a rear set-back of 11 m, the reduction in the depth of the building footprint permits the overall plot depth to be decreased from 23 m to 21 m; however, the overall area of the plot increases. All things being equal this results in a drop in gross density from about 60 dwellings per hectare for the 5 m plot to about 48 dwellings per hectare in the case of the 6 m wide plot.

In general terms, both options are suited to a range of procurement options, including self builders or building cooperative groups (regardless of the arrangement of plots), but neither option is particularly well suited to mixed uses, higher densities or urban-scaled buildings associated with higher townhouse models on narrower plots. This makes them more suited to suburban contexts than urban or peri-urban locations ■

△ Residential perimeter block, Ypenburg,
the Netherlands (West 8 Urban Design
and Landscape Architecture)

◁ Individually designed terrace of
close-grain townhouses, Ijburg, the
Netherlands (various architects)

5.6.3 Close-grain

(mainly residential) perimeter block with rear access lane

This type of block is distinguished by separating the backs of plots with a rear access lane. The resulting plots are effectively 'through plots', because they have frontage onto the street, with access to the rear of the plot being provided from the lane.

This is a common block type in older residential areas. The main advantage of this block type is that secondary access to back gardens is available without having to go through the house. The laneway is also traditionally used for waste storage and collection.

Secured by Design, an initiative by the police to 'design out crime', discourages this type of layout on the basis that the relatively unsupervised laneway makes the plot vulnerable to burglars, especially where wheelie bins and their like offer a platform to vault rear boundary walls.

The vulnerability of the rear access lane to would-be criminals can be circumvented by the inclusion of ancillary accommodation overlooking the lane. This can take the form of live-work units and/or dual occupancy (e.g. a granny flat or mews) with independent access at the rear of the plot.

A byproduct of separating the backs of plots from each other by a laneway is that the overall separation distance between opposing windows can be made up by the combined depth of plots and width of lane, allowing less deep plots to achieve a greater separation distance than longer back-to-back plots.

As with other block types, the corner plot poses the greatest challenge. Whereas in the case of back-to-back configurations it is preferable for plots at the ends of the block to turn the corner (in order to provide frontage on all sides of the block), in the example shown, the inclusion of a live-work and/or mews at the rear of the plot in combination with a plan arrangement for the main dwelling that addresses both frontages allows the block to be terminated without turning

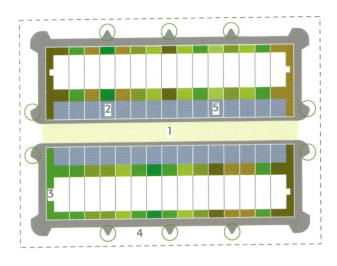

0   10m   20m

◁ Close-grain 'dual aspect' block comprising dwelling houses with rear lane activated by live-work units

1. Rear access lane
2. Lane activated by live-work units
3. Corner plots configured to overlook both frontages
4. On-street parking
5. Potential for on-plot parking but produces 'dead frontage'

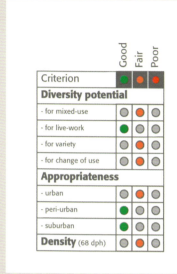

Criterion	Good	Fair	Poor
Diversity potential			
- for mixed-use	○	●	○
- for live-work	●	○	○
- for variety	○	●	○
- for change of use	○	●	○
Appropriateness			
- urban	○	●	○
- peri-urban	●	○	○
- suburban	●	○	○
Density (68 dph)	○	●	○

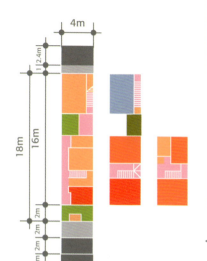

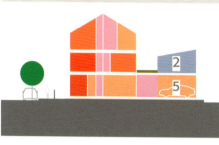

◁ 4 m wide live-work plot with 3-storey townhouse and home office/workshop accessed from rear access lane

the end plots through 90°. This avoids bringing the lane down the length of side gardens, from which it may be more difficult to provide passive surveillance.

In common with the previous examples, parking is provided predominantly on the street, in the case of narrow plots, or in combination with on-plot parking behind the main building line, where sufficient plot width permits. Parking may also be provided under live-work or mews units at the rear. However, the 'dead frontage' associated with garages would undermine the objective to overlook the laneway.

The illustrated 4 m wide plot shows the effect of introducing a rear lane on the depth of plot required to achieve the same separation distance of 22 m as the equivalent back-to-back plot. All other factors being equal, this arrangement can achieve relatively high gross densities of around 68 dwellings per hectare but at the expense of garden space in the middle of the plot being squeezed.

These factors together suggest that this type of block lends itself to live-working, and consequently remains relevant to a range of peri-urban and suburban contexts ■

△ Dual-access plot type in Almere Poort (note party wall insulated pending construction on neighbouring plot)

△ Aerial view of Homeruskwartier West, Almere Poort, the Netherlands, showing detached house plots under construction

5.6.4 Close-grain

(mainly residential) perimeter block with shared courtyard

This variation of the perimeter block combines elements of more conventional block layouts – namely the configuration of private plots facing the street – with the modern apartment block, where the interior of the block is communal.

The short frontage thus faces the street in the conventional way; however, the rear gardens back onto a shared space. Hollowing out the block in this way allows less deep plots to achieve similar or greater separation distances than back-to-back plots. The resulting space has several advantages, particularly the benefit of a large overlooked play space. The shared space also provides the opportunity to incorporate shared services, such as a crèche or other shared communal facilities. However, the resulting increase in the overall size of the block is traded off against the commensurate lowering of density compared with more conventional block types.

The success of the communal space may be compromised by the desire to make rear gardens completely private, because the resulting loss of surveillance may reduce its ability to be self-policing. It is also axiomatic that the cost of maintaining the communal space and any communal facilities imposes an extra charge on its residents.

1. Shared courtyard
2. Potential for shared facilities
3. Corner plots configured to overlook both frontages
4. On-street parking
5. Wider plots permit variety of building types
6. Shared space justifies reduced plot depth but compromises scope for future extension
7. Garden level can be raised to provide privacy, subject to visitable access being provided

0   10m   20m

▷ Close-grain block comprising dwelling houses with central shared open space and shared community facility

△ Close-grain (mainly residential) mews-type perimeter block with shared courtyards and parking courts

1. Shared courtyard
2. Potential for shared facilities
3. Corner plots configured to overlook both frontages
4. On-street parking
5. Wider plots permit variety of building types
6. Shared space justifies reduced plot depth but compromises scope for future extension
7. Garden level can be raised to provide privacy subject to visitable access being provided
8. On-plot parking

In the illustrated examples, less deep plots are compensated for by widening the plots, so that sufficient garden space may be provided without adding unnecessarily to the overall depth of the block. Wider plots also allow a greater variety in housing types to be considered, or the possibility of combining plots of different width that are suitable for row housing, detached and/or semi-detached rows.

As the interior of this type is given over to open space, parking is constrained to the street, except where plots are sufficiently wide to accommodate parking space in side gardens, behind the building line.

The second example of this type combines two blocks in one, with shared vehicular and pedestrian access into the middle of the block allowing incorporation of parking. It thus combines shared communal open spaces in the interior of the block with limited on-site parking. Similar (gross) densities of about 40–45 dwellings per hectare are achievable, and this could be increased to about 50 dwellings per hectare with the inclusion of apartments.

The illustrated plot shows the relationship between a generic 6 m wide house plan and plot depth, given a front set-back of 2 m from the street.

The shallow building footprint achievable with wider plots combined with the increased separation distance provided for by the courtyard (as well as the availability of the courtyard for play and other uses) justifies less deep plots than might otherwise be expected. On the other hand, potential for extending houses to the rear is correspondingly reduced.

The availability of the courtyard for access also opens up the possibility of raising internal ground-floor levels above the level of the street and/or the level of the courtyard itself. This has the advantage of improving privacy on the street as well as the courtyard, without the need to erect physical barriers in the form of fencing. This approach may depend on using the space available at the rear to provide ramped access for the disabled, however.

Although this configuration demands a relatively high level of cooperation between residents and achieves relatively low densities, these factors make it well suited to cooperative building groups and co-housing groups that view communal space and shared facilities as a desirable goal ■

◁ 6 m wide residential plot with 2-storey terraced house overlooking shared internal courtyard

Criterion	Good	Fair	Poor
Diversity potential			
- for mixed-use	○	●	○
- for live-work	○	○	●
- for variety	○	●	○
- for change of use	○	○	●
Appropriateness			
- urban	○	○	●
- peri-urban	○	●	○
- suburban	●	○	○
Density (45 dph)	○	○	●

◁ Interior view of close-grain courtyard block, Waterrijk Woerden, Woerden, the Netherlands (West 8 Urban Design and Landscape Architecture)

▽ Interior view of close-grain block, Sluseholmen, Copenhagen, Denmark (Arkitema Architects)

5.6.5   Close-grain

(mainly residential) perimeter block with double-loaded access

This is a variation of the perimeter block with rear access lane. Instead of plots backing onto the lane, however, it has two rows of back-to-back plots with the inner rows fronting the lane. Though superficially this is the same as two conventional blocks with back-to-back plots arranged side by side, the lane is secondary to the surrounding streets in terms of its place in the wider movement and access hierarchy.

Similar issues arise in the layout and configuration of corner plots here as in the simpler version, specifically the issue of plots turning the corner in order to facilitate overlooking of both streets as well as the lane.

In the example shown, the main street is fronted by long narrow plots backing onto much wider, but less deep, plots. This type of arrangement presupposes that a different type of building typology occupies the plots backing onto each other. In this example, the narrow plots are suited to attached townhouses with on-street car-parking whereas the wider plots can accommodate detached, semi-detached or even detached dwellings with much wider building footprints and space left over for on-plot car-parking behind the building line.

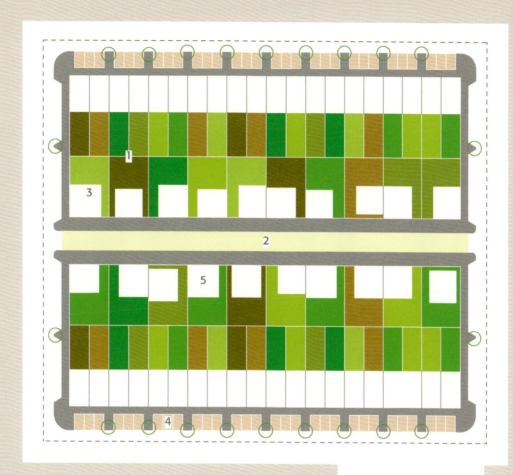

The number of storeys required to achieve a given floor area (plus live-work) in the case of the narrower townhouse plots also makes them necessarily higher than the 'urban villa' type implied by the wider plots. This illustrates how the mixing of plot types, if guided by simple rules, can generate a hierarchy of scale that also mitigates the spatial relationship of one type to another.

For example, if the townhouses are required to incorporate an element of live-work or commercial use on the ground floor, the consequent raising of habitable rooms above ground level simultaneously buffers the townhouse from the street and mitigates the potential for privacy loss between opposing windows at first-floor level.

An interesting precedent for this arrangement is located near Amsterdam at Steigereiland, Ijburg ■

1. Back-to-back plots
2. Mews lane potential as 'homezone'
3. Corner plots configured to overlook both frontages
4. On-street parking
5. Wider plots permit variety of building types

△ Close-grain 'mews type' perimeter block comprising double bank of back-to-back residential/ live-work plots with terraced townhouses and detached mews houses

◁ Aerial view of close-grain townhouses (terraced and detached), Steigereiland, Ijburg, the Netherlands

5.6.6 Close-grain

(mixed-use) hybrid block with through plots

This block type isn't a typical perimeter block because it isn't configured to enclose a private space at the rear in the way most perimeter blocks do. Rather, it is composed of a line of contiguous 'through' plots that extend from one street to the next. Ordinarily, the ambiguity of which side is 'the front' and which side is 'the back' would make this format problematical from an urban design and architectural point of view. In the example shown, however, the plot takes advantage of a change in level to create 'two-faced' plots that perform in a similar way to a conventional perimeter block so that one side is fronted by residential use at upper-ground level while the other side is fronted by a shop or commercial use at lower-ground level.

This typology has successful historical precedents, for example 'The Pantiles' in Tunbridge Wells. It does involve compromises, however, because the light well at the back of the commercial unit is exposed to public view from one side and the private open space serving the residential unit is exposed to public view from the other ■

1. Through plots
2. Active frontage to both sides
3. Corner plots configured to overlook both frontages
4. On-street parking
5. Change in level

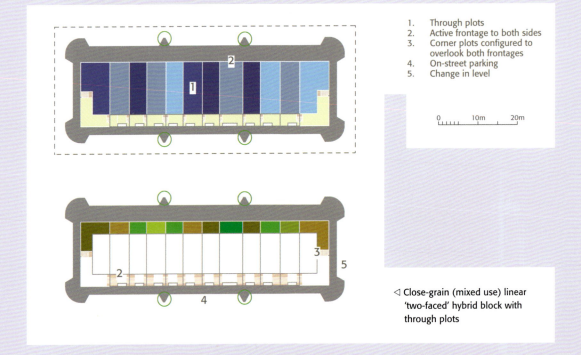

◁ Close-grain (mixed use) linear 'two-faced' hybrid block with through plots

▷ The houses above these shops fronting the Pantiles, Royal Tunbridge Wells, are accessed from another street at the rear of the plots, which runs parallel to the Pantiles but at a higher level

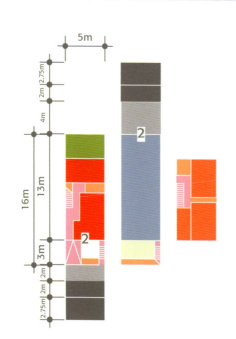

Criterion	Good	Fair	Poor
Diversity potential			
- for mixed-use	●	○	○
- for live-work	●	○	○
- for variety	●	○	○
- for change of use	○	●	○
Appropriateness			
- urban	○	●	○
- peri-urban	●	○	○
- suburban	○	●	○
Density (50 dph)	○	●	○

△ Close-grain mixed-use 'two-faced' through plot with commerical use at lower level and residential use at upper level

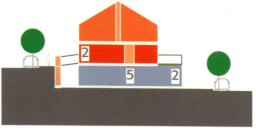

5.6.7 Mixed-grain

(mixed-use) perimeter block with rear access lane

This example splits the block to create a row of close-grain plots on one half of the block with a single large plot on the other half, separated by an access lane.

The close-grain plots are configured to facilitate mixed-use street buildings comprising ground-floor commercial units with apartments overhead: another variant of 'living over the shop'. The large plot is occupied by a conventional block of apartments or mixed uses enclosing a shared courtyard.

The size and shape of the close-grain plots is influenced by the different space requirements of mixed uses. Plot width needs to provide sufficient commercial frontage at ground level for retail purposes with space for separate access and vertical circulation to upper floors from the street. This needs to be balanced with the benefit of maximising the number of frontages along the street. The depth of plots is also influenced by the need to provide sufficient floor space at ground level to accommodate a range of retail (including comparison goods) and commercial uses. This can be supplemented by additional commercial space at basement level accessed from within the unit.

Upper floors may be given over to one dual-aspect apartment per floor, with the potential for the uppermost unit to be a duplex type, permitting an urban scale of building height to be achieved within the constraints of fire regulations. Arranging apartments in a hierarchy of sizes with a larger unit at first-floor level and smaller units above can be taken advantage of to create a cascade of roof terrace gardens.

Upper floors may also be used for commercial (e.g. office) uses; however, two different types of use sharing the same circulation space makes it more difficult to comply with fire

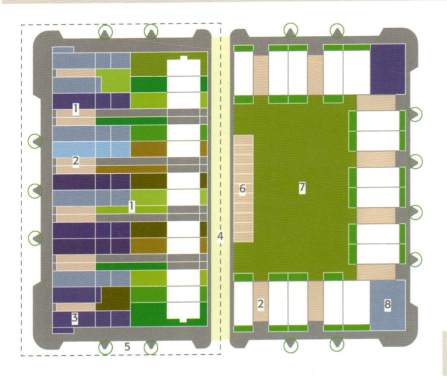

1. Close-grain plot with ground floor/basement commercial uses and apartments above
2. Access from street to upper floors
3. Corner plots configured with sufficient space to overlook both frontages
4. Access lane fronted by mews
5. On-street parking
6. Shared parking
7. Coarse-grain apartment block with shared courtyard and potential basement parking
8. Greatest potential for commercial uses in corner plots

◁ Mixed-grain perimeter 'mews-type' block comprising close-grain mixed-used use commercial and residential apartments with mews houses and coarse-grain apartment block

◁ 6 m wide mixed-use plot with ground floor and basement commerical and residential and/ or office uses overhead, live-work mews overlooking rear access lane

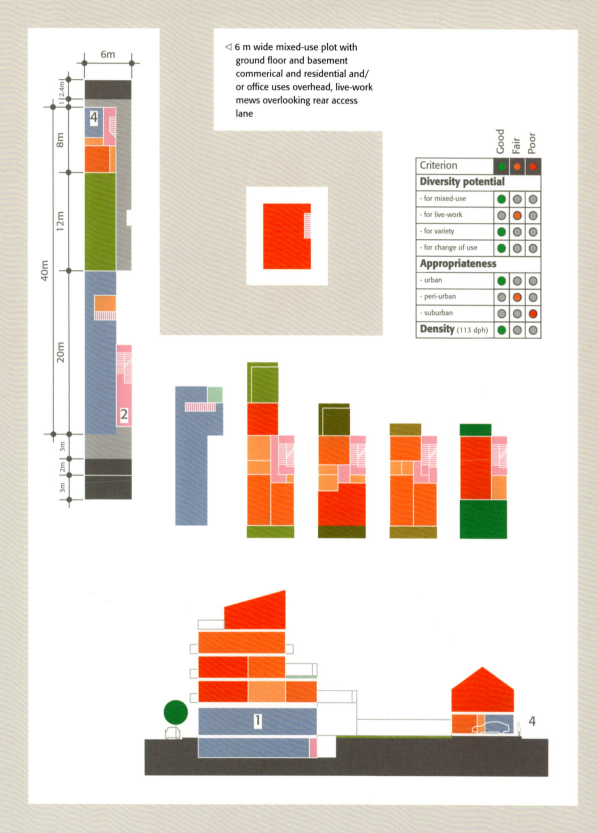

Criterion	Good	Fair	Poor
Diversity potential			
- for mixed-use	🟢	⚪	⚪
- for live-work	⚪	🟠	⚪
- for variety	🟢	⚪	⚪
- for change of use	🟢	⚪	⚪
Appropriateness			
- urban	🟢	⚪	⚪
- peri-urban	⚪	🟠	⚪
- suburban	⚪	⚪	🔴
Density (113 dph)	🟢	⚪	⚪

regulations and, in any case, may cause conflict between them.

The access lane is overlooked by attached mews housing that acts as a buffer between the backs of the commercial uses and the neighbouring courtyard while also facilitating access to them from the rear. The plots can be made sufficiently deep to provide each mews house with a small front set-back and its own rear garden.

In the example shown, the remainder of the block is completed by a conventional apartment block with a shared courtyard. The interior courtyard thus acts as a sort of borrowed landscape shared between the mews houses and the remainder of the block. The conventional courtyard apartment block also has potential for limited mixed-use elements, particularly ground-floor corner units.

As with all perimeter blocks, corner units provide a particular challenge: providing a layout that satisfactorily addresses both frontages on the outside without unduly stifling the inside angle. In practice, the simplest solution is to provide wider plots at corners, making it easier for buildings to turn the corner, and using the circulation space to provide 'breathing room' inside. This is achieved in the example illustrated by making corner plots wide enough to provide two units per floor with a shared access core.

Car-parking is provided mainly on the street, making this option appropriate to urban locations where there is sufficient critical mass to justify greater reliance on public transport. If the close-grain and coarse-grain elements of the block are constructed jointly, however, there may be an opportunity to provide shared basement car-parking space under the courtyard block.

In broad terms, this type of block and plot configuration is particularly suited to the creation of new urban centres where it is desirable to create a varied and interesting streetscape with sufficient critical mass to support a range of different uses ■

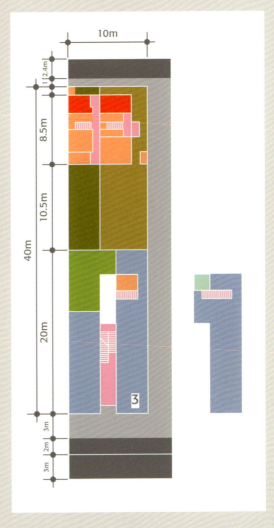

◁ 10 m wide mixed-use corner
plot with commercial use of
ground floor and basement
and residential (or office) uses
overhead. Potential for live-work
mews overlooking rear access
lane

Criterion	Good	Fair	Poor
Diversity potential			
- for mixed-use	●	○	○
- for live-work	○	●	○
- for variety	●	○	○
- for change of use	●	○	○
Appropriateness			
- urban	●	○	○
- peri-urban	○	●	○
- suburban	○	○	●
Density (113 dph)	●	○	○

5.6.8 Medium-grain

(mainly residential) perimeter block with shared courtyard

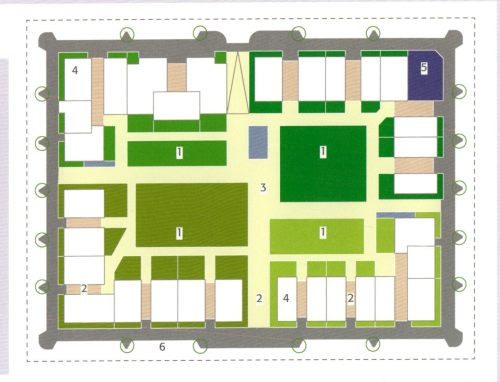

0   10m   20m

△ Medium-grain mixed-use
perimeter block with communal
courtyard comprising mainly
apartments but with potential
for commercial uses on ground
floors, especially at corners

1.   Medium-grain apartment
     buildings by different designers
2.   Access from street to shared
     courtyard and upper floors
3.   Shared courtyard, basement and
     facilities
4.   Corners configured to overlook
     both frontages
5.   Greatest potential for
     commercial uses at corners
6.   On-street parking

Superficially, this is a conventional form of perimeter block. However, it is included to illustrate the potential to create diversity and variety by procuring different developers and/or different architects to design different parts of the same block.

This doesn't divide the block into separate plots *per se* because it allows different buildings to share the same courtyard space and underground parking, waste management facilities, and the like. However, it can create the same degree of diversity and variety as if the block had been so divided. This, in turn, requires a cooperative approach to developing the block as a whole, because it must be

Criterion	Good	Fair	Poor
Diversity potential			
- for mixed-use	🟢	⚪	⚪
- for live-work	🟢	⚪	⚪
- for variety	⚪	🟠	⚪
- for change of use	⚪	🟠	⚪
Appropriateness			
- urban	🟢	⚪	⚪
- peri-urban	⚪	🟠	⚪
- suburban	⚪	⚪	🔴
Density (120+ dph)	🟢	⚪	⚪

△ Indicative medium-grain plot showing one approach to apartments turning the corner, while also providing access from the street as well as through access from the street to a shared courtyard

overseen by a coordinating agent and a coordinating architect. This approach is commonplace in Sweden, for example.

The example shown thus comprises four stand-alone apartment buildings each occupying approximately one quarter of the block. Each group of apartments is notionally designed by a different architect. Depending on the economies of scale needed to generate interest by a given scale of developer, parts of the block could be allocated to a smaller or greater number of different interests.

The plan arrangement at corners of apartment blocks is more challenging than in simple close-grain residential blocks because service cores serving apartments, which are usually higher than townhouses, are more likely to need lift access. The desire to limit the number of apartments per floor needs to be reconciled with the cost per unit of providing and maintaining the lift by future residents, which in turn, depends on the overall number of units served by the lift. This is discussed in more detail in Chapter 6.

Many and varied plan arrangements are possible. However, it is in practice difficult to serve more than three apartments per floor without introducing at least one single-aspect unit. Serving four apartments invariable means including one single-aspect unit (not counting corner units), and serving more than four usually means introducing longer corridors and/or shared deck access, which is not usually favoured in the UK or Ireland.

Whatever plan arrangement is chosen, in order to ensure that as much activity remains focused on the street as possible all entrances should be accessible from the street. They should also preferably permit through access from the street to the courtyard and vice versa.

The densities achievable with this form of development are effectively the same as for apartment blocks developed by a single developer. This makes them suitable for urban areas.

The availability of basement car-parking for residents also eases demand for on-street space, making provision for live-work practices and limited commercial uses more feasible.

The degree of variety and interest made possible by involving more than one designer makes this approach more visually interesting and provides greater choice to the market than equivalent 'homogenised' blocks, but the scale of each component of the block effectively limits the number of different parties that can reasonably be expected to participate. This, in turn, limits the degree of variety and scope for change compared with close-grain blocks ■

△ Interior of medium-grain block,
   Sluseholmen, Copenhagen, Denmark
   (Arkitema Architects)

△ Exterior of mixed-grain block,
Sluseholmen, Copenhagen, Denmark
(Arkitema Architects)

5.6.9 Close-grain

(mixed-use) perimeter block with shared podium courtyard

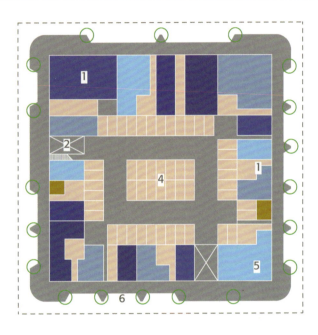

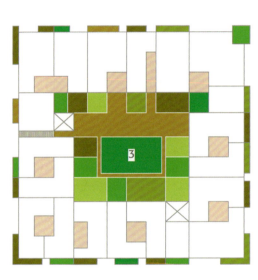

0   10m   20m

1. Close-grain mixed-use buildings by different developers/designers
2. Access from street to shared courtyard and upper floors
3. Shared podium courtyard
4. Shared parking garage with access to back of commercial units
5. Corners configured to overlook both frontages
6. On-street parking

△ Close-grain mixed-use perimeter block with shared podium courtyard

This type shares key features with both the close-grain courtyard block and the conventional or medium-grain perimeter block, specifically a close grain of individual plots and a shared courtyard respectively. The fundamental difference, which it also shares with traditional urban blocks, is that it is composed of a variety of plot widths, all with commercial uses at ground level and residential and/or compatible commercial uses overhead.

Pioneering precedents for this exist in Tübingen Südstadt in Germany and in the Homeruskwartier centre of Almere Poort, near Amsterdam (under construction).

In the case of Almere the basic block parameters are set out together with ground rules for front and rear building lines, height, and so on. However, no plot subdivision is imposed. Rather, the individual project proponents choose their own

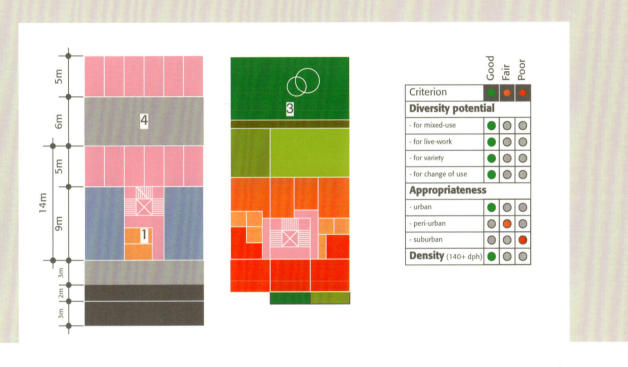

Criterion	Good	Fair	Poor
Diversity potential			
- for mixed-use	🟢	⚪	⚪
- for live-work	🟢	⚪	⚪
- for variety	🟢	⚪	⚪
- for change of use	🟢	⚪	⚪
Appropriateness			
- urban	🟢	⚪	⚪
- peri-urban	⚪	🟠	⚪
- suburban	⚪	⚪	🔴
Density (140+ dph)	🟢	⚪	⚪

△ Close-grain mixed-use plot with
   shared podium courtyard

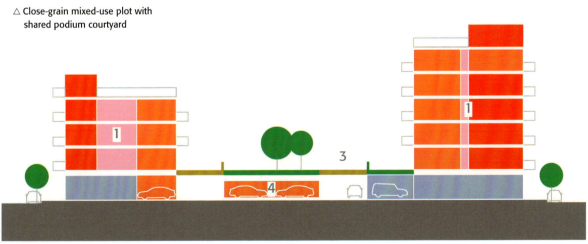

△ Oblique aerial view of close-/medium-
grain mixed-use perimeter block in
Tübingen Südstadt, Germany

▷ Illustrative proposal for a mixed-grain
block, Dublin

plot on a first come, first served basis, subject to a maximum permissible commercial floor space. This latter stipulation is designed to prevent larger commercial chains dominating the centre, but it also keeps plot sizes down, thus maximising the potential for variety and mixed uses to occur. The municipality is then responsible for ensuring that any residual plots left over are workable and that corner plots are not unduly constrained.

The example shown extrapolates this idea in diagrammatic form to illustrate the potential for a range of different buildings and uses to populate the block incrementally, while retaining the benefits of shared space for car-parking and access to the rear of ground floor commercial units as well as shared courtyard space for residents.

The Almere authority has branded this approach 'the Tübingen model', where project groups were also required to include commercial uses at ground level.

The example shows how a typical plot could be developed with two commercial units at ground level separated by vertical circulation serving two residential units per floor overhead, accessible both from the street and from the rear

parking court. This podium arrangement allows unsightly 'back-of-house' elements such as parking to be concealed directly behind the ground-floor commercial units without the costly excavation of basement space, while first-floor apartments open directly on the courtyard.

The potential for variation in design, layout and arrangement of plots within the block's parameters is limited only by the imagination and ingenuity of its designers.

The purchase of mixed-use plots in Almere Poort includes a share in the courtyard and parking garage, which are constructed by the municipality and are subsequently owned and managed in common-hold by the users.

The incorporation of mixed uses, variety and incremental change together with relatively high densities makes this option eminently suited to new urban centres with a sufficient population threshold to make them viable. In reality, new urban areas take time to 'bed in' and to achieve critical mass. A flexible approach needs to be adopted during the bedding in period to keep plot prices low and to allow ground-floor units to be temporarily occupied for residential use ■

5.6.10 Medium-grain

(mixed-use) perimeter block

This example is composed of individual discrete plots, without any communal space in the interior of the block. As a result, it more closely resembles a traditional urban block than the previous example. Subdividing the block into back-to-back plots requires each plot to be accessed from the street; however, if a service yard or on-plot parking is required this must also be taken from the street. This reduces the available commercial frontage, which is also eroded by access to the upper floors. As in the case of the examples of residential blocks with rear access, the introduction of a service lane can overcome these issues. However, it also raises issues of overlooking and security, which in the case of potentially high-value retail outlets may outweigh the potential benefits (unless the lane is gated).

In the illustrative example shown, the block is made up of a relatively small number of back-to-back plots. The mid-row plots are sufficiently large to accommodate one wide com-mercial frontage or two smaller ones separated by vertical access to the upper floors. Corner plots are larger, to allow buildings to 'turn' the corner.

As with the previous mixed-use block, the relatively high density required to create a critical mass of population to support a range of different uses together with the lack of shared basement car-parking makes it more appropriate to central urban locations than peri-urban or suburban locations and also assumes sufficient numbers of units per plot, compared with smaller close-grain plots, to justify lift access to upper floors.

In the example shown, mid-row plots are wide enough to accommodate two or three residential units per floor (e.g. two dual-aspect units plus one single-aspect unit). Corner plots are sized to accommodate up to four units per floor. As in the case of conventional apartment blocks, however,

◁ 3D sketch proposal for a mixed-grain block, Dublin

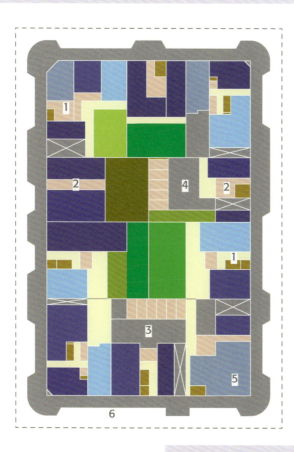

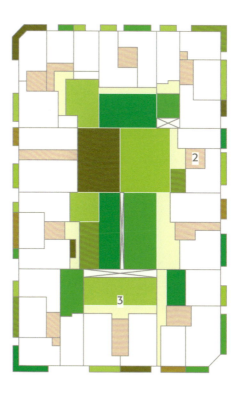

0   10m   20m

△ Close-grain mixed-use perimeter block with individual 'single-aspect' (back-to-back) plots

1. Medium-grain plots with mixed-use buildings by different developers/designers
2. Access from street to courtyard and/or upper floors
3. Potential for shared podium courtyard with undercroft parking
4. Shared on-plot parking with access to back of commercial units
5. Corners configured to overlook both frontages
6. On-street parking

▷ Example of a mixed-use 'mansion' type block in London (Porphyrios Associates)

△ Infill development of 'mansion' type
mixed-use apartments and shops at
Highbury Gardens, London
(Porphyrios Associates)

there is a limit to how many units per floor can be served by a single access core without introducing corridors, more single-aspect units and/or deck access.

Provided stair cores give way to the rear, the residual open space may be shared between the residents or divided between residents and ground-floor uses. Alternatively, it may be decked to provide undercroft parking/service yard with amenity space at first-floor level.

This type of block and plot arrangement is similar to the tried and tested mansion typology found in London or the post-Haussmann blocks found in Paris. These were usually spacious apartments (often two per floor) designed for the new middle class; however, their versatility and adaptability confers on them a continued relevance today. The mansion type is championed by the Prince's Foundation for the Built Environment, and there are a number of precedents for its revival (e.g. Highbury Gardens by Porphyrios Associates, developed by First Base, near Islington in London) ■

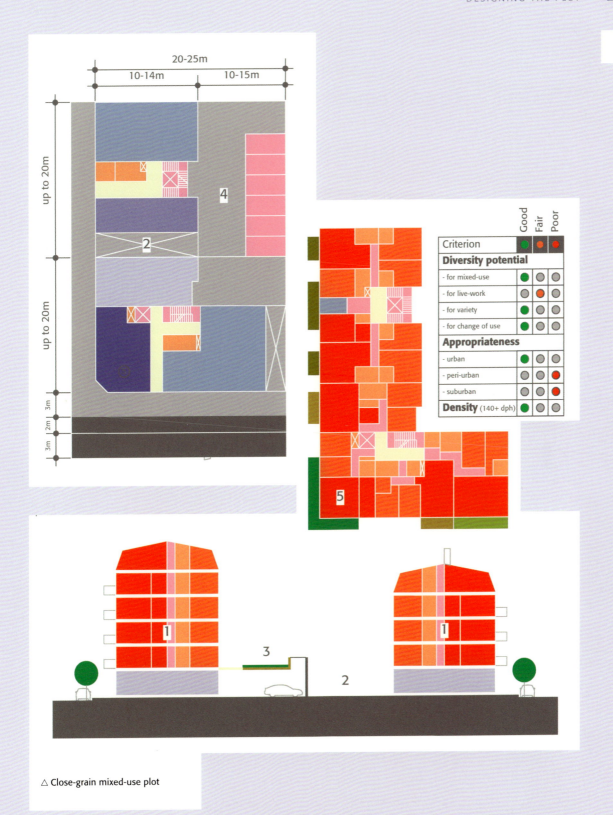

Criterion	Good	Fair	Poor
Diversity potential			
- for mixed-use	🟢	⚪	⚪
- for live-work	⚪	🟠	⚪
- for variety	🟢	⚪	⚪
- for change of use	🟢	⚪	⚪
Appropriateness			
- urban	🟢	⚪	⚪
- peri-urban	⚪	⚪	🔴
- suburban	⚪	⚪	🔴
Density (140+ dph)	🟢	⚪	⚪

△ Close-grain mixed-use plot

5.6.11   Ready reckoner

BUILDING TYPE	PLOT TYPE		RESIDENTIAL UNITS PER PLOT	COMMERCIAL UNITS PER PLOT	UNIT WIDTH (INTERNAL)
Row housing	Back to back	Single-aspect plots	1 single-family dwelling	Potential for live-work	4.0 m
					5.0 m
					6.0 m
	Back to side	Corner plots	1 single-family dwelling	Potential for live-work	4.0 m
					5.0 m
					6.0 m
	Back to lane	Dual-aspect plots	1 single-family dwelling	Potential for live-work	4.0 m
	Back to court		1 single-family dwelling	Potential for live-work	6.0 m
Semi-detached housing	Back to back	Single-aspect plots	1 single-family dwelling	Potential for live-work	4.0 m
			1 single-family dwelling		5.0 m
			1 single-family dwelling		6.0 m
Mixed-use (residential over commercial)	Double fronted	Dual-aspect plots	1 single-family dwelling	1 commercial unit	4.0 m
			1 single-family dwelling	1 commercial unit	5.0 m
			1 single-family dwelling	1 commercial unit	6.0 m
Mixed-use (apartments or offices over commercial)	Back to lane	Dual-aspect plots	2+ apartments (1 apartment per floor)	1+ commercial unit(s)	6.0 m
		Corner plots	4+ apartments (2 apartments per floor)	2+ commercial unit(s)	10.0 m
Mixed-use (apartments or offices over commercial) with mews housing	Back to lane	Dual-aspect plots	2+ apartments 1 mews dwelling (1 apartment per floor)	1+ commercial unit(s)	6.0 m
Mixed-use (mainly apartments)	N/A	Corner (quadrant) plots	35+ to 45+ apartments (2–4 units per core)	1+ commercial unit(s)	5.0 m–7.0 m
Mixed-use (apartments or offices over commercial)	Back to back	Single-aspect plots	8+ to 12+ apartments (2–3 apartments per floor)	2+ commercial units	15.0 m–20.0 m
	Back to side	Corner plots	12+ to 16+ apartments (3–4 apartments per floor)	3+ commercial units	15.0 m–25.0 m

UNIT DEPTH (INTERNAL)	BUILDING HEIGHT	PLOT WIDTH	PLOT DEPTH	INDICATIVE DENSITY RANGE (GROSS) [†]	APPROPRIATENESS
8.5 m	3+ storeys	4.30 m	21.5 m	50 dph to 60+ dph	Suburban/peri-urban
10.0 m	2+ storeys	5.30 m	23.0 m	50 dph	
8.0 m	2+ storeys	6.30 m	21.0 m	40 dph to 50 dph	
8.5 m	3+ storeys	6.15 m	19.5 m	–	
10.0 m	2+ storeys	7.15 m	21.0 m	–	
8.0 m	2+ storeys	8.15 m	19.0 m	–	
8.5 m	3+ storeys	4.30 m	18.0 m	60 dph to 70 dph	
8.0 m	2+ storeys	6.30 m	16.0 m	40 dph to 45 dph	
8.5 m	3+ storeys	7.15 m	21.5 m	40 dph to 45 dph	Suburban
10.0 m	2+ storeys	8.15 m	23.0 m	35 dph to 45 dph	
8.0 m	2+ storeys	9.15 m	21.0 m	30 dph to 35 dph	
8.5 m	4+ storeys	4.30 m	15.25 m	70 dph	Peri-urban
10.0 m	3+ storeys	5.30 m	16.0 m	55 dph	
8.0 m	3+ storeys	6.30 m	13.5 m	50 dph	
20.0 m	3+ storeys	6.30 m	20.0 m	90 dph to 135 dph	Urban/peri-urban
20.0 m (ground) 10.0 m–14.0 m (upper)	3+ storeys	10.15 m	20.0 m		
20.0 m	3+ storeys	6.30 m	40.0 m	100 dph to 110 dph	
10.0 m–14.0 m	5+ storeys	50.0 m	35.0 m	150+ dph	
10.0 m–12.0 m	5+ storeys	15.3 m–20.3 m	20.0 m–25.0 m	170+ dph	Urban
10.0 m–12.0 m	5+ storeys	15.15 m–20.15 m	20.0 m–25.0 m		

Ready reckoner for blocks and plots

The ready reckoner extracts critical information from the diagrammatic examples of blocks and plots, and presents it in tabular form as a supplementary aid to design. The table allows the masterplanner to see at a glance the relationship between different building typologies and plot sizes, and the implications of these for density, building height, mix of uses and so on.

The purpose of the ready reckoner is to provide a simple means of testing the viability of plots for different uses and densities, and, ultimately, a basis for developing a masterplan that is robust enough for detailed proposals relating to *individual* plots to be brought forward by multiple designers later on. As such, it is not intended to impose standards, *per se*, but to provide guidance as to the size and shape of plots that are sufficient to accommodate various building typologies.

† As discussed in Chapter 2, the calculation of density is problematic for several reasons, particularly gross density, because the amount of land-take for streets, open spaces and non-residential uses can vary a great deal. The densities indicated in this table are based on the illustrative block and plot examples shown in this chapter and, as such, take account of street widths and non-residential uses within the block, but not parks or other significant land uses (e.g. churches) that are external to the block. The wide range of densities indicated in some cases in the table arises because there is also a great deal of scope for variation in the area of open space *within* certain kinds of blocks (especially courtyard blocks) as well as in building height, especially where passenger lifts are provided.

5.6.12   Testing the plot

Once the overall urban structure and block layout has been determined, the size and shape of blocks should be stress-tested to ensure that they are robust enough to accommodate the nature and extent of diversity that the masterplan is seeking to achieve in the short, medium and long terms.

Stress-testing involves checking the physical and economic viability of blocks and plots with regard to their capacity for development, potential mix of uses and sensitivity to market conditions. CABE[126] suggests the minimum capacity necessary to achieve a sense of place and the minimum catchments required for the range of uses and services envisaged also needs to be defined, and recommends that blocks and plots should be tested to ensure that:

☐ plots make sense in relation to the likely sizes and shapes of buildings

☐ the proposed land uses can be accommodated

☐ open space and amenity at the level of the plot and block will be sufficient

☐ the blocks and plots indicated correspond with what developers will want to build

☐ permeability around and through blocks is achieved

☐ the effects of built form and massing on sunlight, microclimate and views have been considered.

This exercise needs to take place iteratively as more detailed information becomes available and as design progresses from concept-stage masterplanning through to more detailed site layout planning for individual blocks and the public realm. In the first instance, the emerging masterplan should be reviewed internally as part of the quality management regime to make sure that the overall urban and landscape structure is satisfactory and that blocks and plots are 'fit for purpose' within the limits of the information known at the time.

The table of plot sizes can be used as a ready reckoner to assist in this process by ensuring that plots and blocks intended for specific purposes (e.g. mixed-use street buildings or row housing) are appropriately sized for those purposes, and that they are likely to meet density targets.

Following this initial check, two-dimensional sections and three-dimensional massing studies of key streets and blocks should be generated. These can quickly expose potential issues such as whether density targets are realistic and whether they are compatible with achieving the desired relationships between the width and height of streets and public spaces. They can also be used to confirm, for example, that there is sufficient space in the interior of blocks to meet open space requirements, and that adequate sunlight and daylight can be provided.

As the client's brief hardens, for example as potential tenants or subsidiary developers come on board, the masterplan (or first-phase elements) will need to be revisited to ensure that the specific types of uses can be accommodated and all ancillary requirements, such as access and parking, can be met. This is particularly important where the masterplan is to be submitted as a planning application (whether outline or full), because the granting of permission will effectively 'fix' the main elements of the masterplan, including the footprints, heights and uses of specific buildings.

In complex cases, especially where phasing and/or the requirements of different landowners or developers have to be coordinated, it may be necessary to undertake an intermediate level of masterplanning that is more detailed than the overall masterplan but less detailed than site layout planning. Bridging the gap between broad masterplanning and more detailed design in this way can provide the necessary confidence that different parcels or phases can be properly coordinated and that key infrastructure necessary to link different parts together can be fixed at the appropriate level of detail, before fixing plot boundaries themselves ■

6 Detailing the plot

The aim of plot-based urbanism in general, and plot-based masterplanning in particular, is to foster the characteristics of older close-grain places that we value – diversity, variety, adaptability – while also putting in place the frameworks necessary to achieve all the other objectives of urban design that masterplanning currently prioritises: character, continuity and enclosure, legibility, ease of movement.

Contemporary masterplanning practice tries to achieve these objectives through detailed urban design guidance – design coding – of some kind or another. This starts with the premise that new development can be regulated by the application of certain rules or principles, and that these can be applied and interpreted for a given location and then captured in diagrammatic and written form.[127]

Design codes typically comprise a masterplan, articulated in two and three dimensions, together with a set of written requirements explaining the masterplan (including key dimensions affecting built form, streets and spaces, etc.), materiality or other forms of design prescription. Design coding that neglects the significance of the plot, however, implicitly frames the development of the area in question as a product that can be created and recreated rather than as an incremental process. Developments delivered in this way often result in carefully controlled yet ultimately contrived urban environments lacking any real sense of character or authenticity.

Plot-based approaches to masterplanning differ from conventional approaches by providing for the subdivision of blocks into discrete plots that can be developed individually over time by different developers, in unison by cooperative groups, or in harmony by combinations of larger developers working in partnership with smaller ones, rather than landed by a single agency in the manner of a stage set.

This approach – platting – sets out the plots themselves, while limiting design rules to simpler parameters such as the building envelope. As Campbell explains, adopting simple rules can generate complex results, and the freedoms they confer 'are decisive for the generation of ephemeral qualities such as urban diversity, difference and vitality'.[128]

Design codes, whether they are given effect by a grant of outline planning permission, a separately agreed document, supplementary planning guidance, Local Development Order or Neighbourhood Development Order (see Chapter 4) can thus be used as a tool to front-load the development control process, enabling the development of individual plots to proceed with minimal intervention, subject to an agreed masterplan.

This chimes with the National Planning Policy Framework, which suggests that design codes should avoid unnecessary prescription or detail, focusing instead on scale and massing generally,[129] and with CABE's advice contained in *The Use of Urban Design Codes*, which 'favours codes that ensure we get the fundamentals right but are not so prescriptive that they give too little scope for distinctive architectural expression'.[130] In this context CABE makes special reference to the code for Vauban, near Freiburg in Germany, which established building lines, heights, plot coverage and energy efficiency, but allowed almost complete freedom in other respects.

The challenge, then, is to formulate an appropriate level of coding for a range of plot typologies that, in conjunction with the overall arrangement of plots set out in the masterplan, will allow their intrinsic potential to emerge freely within defined limits while simultaneously advancing the wider objectives of urban design to create good places. This requires a different approach to regulating development than the conventional design code, for which three interrelated tools are needed:

- ☐ the cadastral masterplan
- ☐ the rules for building on each plot type
- ☐ the rules for coordination between plots.

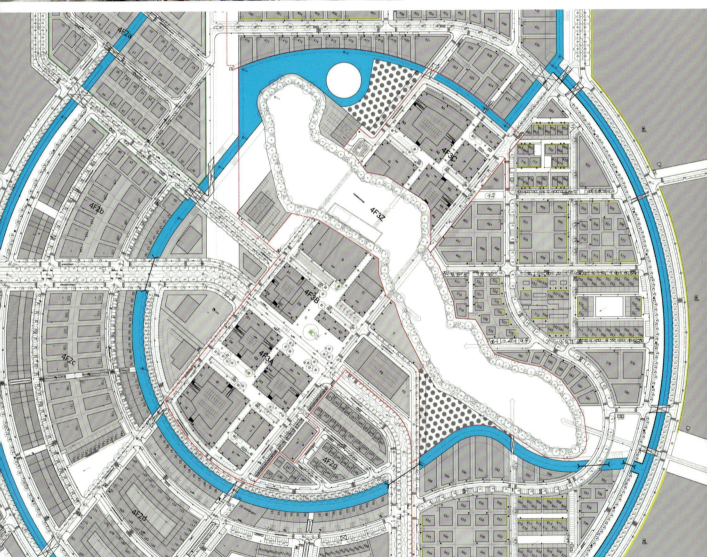

△ Plot plan for Homeruskwartier in Almere Poort, the Netherlands (OMA Architects)

△△ Aerial view showing individual self-build plots being developed on an incremental basis

6.1 THE CADASTRAL MASTERPLAN

The cadastral masterplan, or plot plan, is an extra layer of information on top of the conventional masterplan, which sets out the subdivision of each block in the masterplan into discrete plots that can be offered for sale. Plots may be designated for different building typologies, such as townhouses, detached and semi-detached houses, apartments or mixed-use street buildings.

The plot plan –referred to as a platting map (US), subdivision plan (Australia), *bebauungspläne*[131] (Germany) or *kavelkaart* (Netherlands)– can be colour coded to identify plot types and to cross-reference the location of individual plots with more detailed information regulating the rules for building affecting each plot type as well as plot-specific details.

Almere Poort, near Amsterdam, is currently being developed on this basis according to a programme entitled *Ik bouw mijn huis in Almere* ('I build my house in Almere'). The district as whole is thus laid out according to an overall masterplan comprising six distinct quarters. Each quarter is intended to be developed with its own unique character, which is supplemented by an overall plot plan or 'kavelkaart'. There are approximately 720 individual building plots in each district plus a higher-density centre (Homeruskwartier Centrum) comprising close-grain mixed-use blocks of shops and apartments where the size of plot is chosen by the prospective buyer or building cooperative.[132]

6.2 RULES FOR BUILDING

The rationale for setting out rules for building in the form of a design code is based on the presumption that development proposals which comply with the rules can be allowed to proceed without recourse to normal development control procedures: either without planning permission, or with minimal involvement of the local planning authority.

6.2.1 The building envelope

The purpose of defining a building envelope is to set the physical limits of future buildings in three dimensions, including their relationship to the street and to neighbouring buildings. It is defined by a combination of several parameters: the front building line, building height, building depth and rear building set-back, the width of the plot itself, and the scope of permitted deviations.

All of these are, to a greater or lesser extent, interdependent. They are also influenced by the range of more strategic design considerations discussed in the preceding chapter relating to the type and configuration of the block itself as well as the range of building typologies (detached or semi-detached dwellings, row housing or townhouses, mixed-use street buildings, apartments, etc.) appropriate to it. In addition, they must be supplemented at the more detailed level by considerations of privacy, sunlight and daylight, vertical circulation, parking, access and services.

Front building line

The front building line is the line formed by building façades facing the street. This is sometimes referred to as the 'street wall'. The position of the front building line in relation to the back of the public footpath is a critical factor determining the interface between building uses and the street, especially at ground-floor level. As explained in *By Design*, successful urban streets and spaces are enclosed by buildings, structures or landscape elements. Buildings that follow a continuous building line around a block and contain the private space within the back yards or courtyards help to distinguish between public and private space while also helping to monitor the street.

Factors influencing the front building line are equally relevant to a wide range of plot widths and uses. However, the amount of set-back can have a relatively greater knock-on effect on the depth of narrow plots.

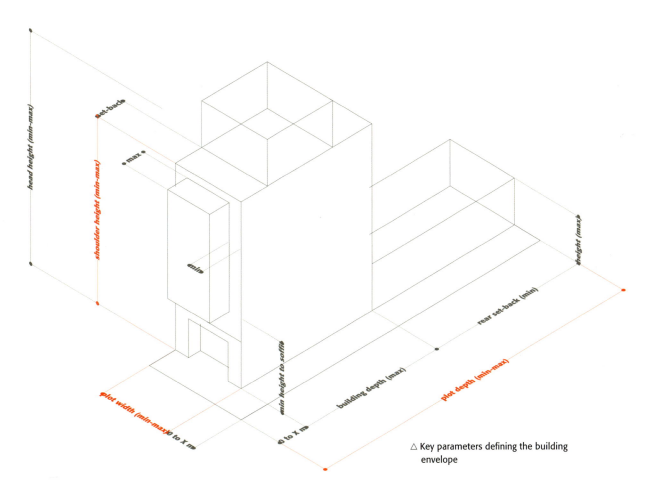

head height (min-max)

set-back

shoulder height (min-max)

max

min

min height to soffit

height (max)

rear set-back (min)

plot width (min-max)

0 to X m

building depth (max)

plot depth (min-max)

△ Key parameters defining the building envelope

Most commercial premises – particularly shops – are purposefully designed to invite people to enter the building directly from the street, or at least be tempted to do so by the attractiveness of the goods or services on display. The principal implications of this from an urban design point of view are that the front building line of mixed-use street buildings should directly address the street, and that separate-level threshold access should be provided to ground-floor commercial units and to vertical circulation spaces serving upper floors.

Conversely, the design of threshold spaces in mixed-use buildings is also important in encouraging activities to 'spill out' onto the street. Use of the public footpath for commercial purposes, such as alfresco dining, are usually licensed by the local authority. This needs to be managed on an ongoing basis. The challenge involves creating a successful balance between the benefits of street life and the potential disbenefits of causing an obstruction to passers-by. This also needs to be considered at the masterplanning stage, to ensure that footpaths will be sufficiently wide to avoid the creation of bottlenecks. Detailed guidance on movement and access issues is contained in the *Manual for Streets*.[133]

Thresholds for residential uses at ground-floor level are more problematic because the desirability of promoting interaction between residents and the street as well as between neighbours needs to be balanced with the need to create a sense of privacy and security, along with provision for bin storage, access to utility meters, bicycle parking, car-parking and so on.

Consequently, it is considered good practice for ground-floor residential uses to be set back from the street, at least sufficiently to create 'defensible space' between the dwelling and the public realm (see section 2.2.4). Determining the appropriate set-back distance is not straightforward, however, because the house buyer's preference for large set-backs and for parking cars in the front garden does not accord with the objectives of urban design to generate sustainable urban densities, a sense of continuity and enclosure, and an intimate relationship between buildings and the street. All this space at the front of the building eats into the amount of space left over to accommodate the building itself and space at the rear and, in turn, affects the relationship between the building and those around it.

CABE considers the house buyer's relationship with the street to be one of the most 'intractable' areas surrounding house design. Specifically, it cites tensions between the desirability of walkable neighbourhoods with a strong sense of community on the one hand, and the competing desire for security (of the private realm), privacy and parking on the other.

Safer Places does not provide guidelines for set-backs, focusing instead on the need to clearly define territory and to provide natural surveillance.[134] The *Urban Design Compendium* recommends set-backs of 1.5 m to 3 m in inner urban areas (including spill-out space for commercial uses) and up to 5 m for outer urban areas (for buffering against busy arterial roads), while also suggesting that this space should not be used for car hard-standings.

According to CABE's survey, only 1% of buyers said that they would accept no front set-back and only 20% would accept less than 1.8 m. The desire for security and privacy in the front garden also needs to be offset against the wider desire for buildings to overlook streets, however.

It is suggested on this basis that a front set-back of 2 m is a robust starting point for masterplanning purposes, because it is large enough to engender neighbourly contact as well as to provide a 'defensible' space, space for utilities and a buffer from the street (particularly if raised above the street level). At the same time, it is small enough to discourage on-plot car-parking in front of the building line while also facilitating a strong sense of enclosure and security of the public realm. Where reduced or zero set-backs are desirable, for example in central locations, domestic uses can still be protected from the street by incorporating live-work spaces at ground level.

The street should be overlooked by main habitable rooms in preference to bedrooms, bathrooms or kitchens. Side streets should also be overlooked and blank gables avoided. Detailing of downpipes, vents and extracts associated with balconies and servant spaces should be carefully considered to ensure that they do not create a mess of visual clutter.

Building height

Determining the appropriate front building line or front set-back for different building typologies requires consideration of both regulatory and perceptual considerations relating to building height. These considerations are by no means unique to close-grain typologies, but some of the considerations have proportionally greater effect on narrow buildings with small floor plates as compared to larger ones.

In order to create a sense of enclosure, building massing should be concentrated towards the street. The height of buildings should relate to the width and status of the streets and spaces they enclose, as well as the degree to which they will overlook and overshadow public and private spaces. Guidance on street width-to-height ratios is provided in the *Urban Design Compendium*, which suggests a width-to-height ratio ranging between 1:1.5 (minimum) and 1:3 (maximum) for streets, and a ratio of between 1:1 (minimum) and 1:1.5 (maximum) for mews lanes.[135] Reduced

△ △ 'Homezone' street in Vauban, Freiburg

△ Live-work housing at Newhall, Harlow
(Proctor and Matthews Architects)

width-to-height ratios may be preferred from the point of view of creating a greater sense of enclosure in certain circumstances, but these must be balanced against reduced access to sunlight and daylight, particularly to lower floors.

Although the *Compendium* does not give specific guidance for homezones (residential streets that typically have narrower, shared surface carriageways with pedestrian and cycle priority), guidance in the *Manual for Streets* relating to 'lightly trafficked' streets suggests that carriageways 4.1 m to 4.8 m wide can allow two cars to pass or a car and a lorry to pass respectively.[136] The absence of a separate footpath in this situation thus reduces the overall width of the street, because the same width is shared by both cars and pedestrians. In turn, this affects the relationship between the front set-back and building height that will achieve a given width-to-height ratio.

Notwithstanding that guidance on street enclosure ratios is somewhat generic (and is irrespective of urban grain), it is unlikely (but not inconceivable) that close-grain building types will not be able to meet the street width-to-height ratios recommended in the *Urban Design Compendium*, despite the relatively limited height they can achieve without lifts being provided.

As outlined in Chapter 5, building height is also influenced by building regulations, which have particular ramifications for the height of buildings on close-grain – that is, narrow – plots, particularly mixed-use and commercial buildings. In essence, the difficulty pertaining to smaller plots arises from the relatively high cost per unit of providing vertical circulation combined with the lack of space available for vertical circulation relative to the amount of usable space left over.

Part M1 of the Building Regulations for England and Wales 2010 (amended 2011), for example, requires reasonable provision to be made for people to gain access to and use buildings and their facilities.[137] The explanatory notes contained in Approved Document M (ADM) make it clear that passenger lifts are the preferred form of access for people moving from one storey to another and should be provided wherever possible, but they acknowledge that such provision might not always be possible.

Levitt, however, explains that to be financially viable (and affordable to maintain), it is necessary for one passenger lift to serve between 10 and 15 dwellings.[138] On first reading, ADM might thus appear to sound the death knell for close-grain typologies because they typically serve just one unit per level. It should be borne in mind, however, that the principal purpose of the Approved Documents is to provide advice on meeting the regulations, and not to prescribe the criteria on which proposals are judged to have met them

or what is considered reasonable. Local Authority Building Control (LABC) Technical Guidance Note *Guide to Vertical Circulation in Non Domestic Buildings* points out that each application should be judged on its merits and this is one of the reasons that Access Statements were introduced. The guidance note lists a number of factors considered relevant to deciding whether it is reasonable to provide a lift (or what type of lift should be provided):

☐ access is to one or two floors only and the area is limited
☐ occupancy/floor space factors are low
☐ the building does not exceed three storeys
☐ floor space does not contain a unique facility
☐ the constraints of the building, particularly if it is of historic interest
☐ means of escape provision may not be achieved owing to floor space/layout constraints
☐ members of the public are not permitted on the floor
☐ nature of business precludes the employment of persons with significant ambulatory difficulties
☐ provision has been made for easy installation of a lift in the future
☐ there is effective full-time management in place
☐ the cost of a passenger lift in relation to the overall project cost is high.

Although there is an expectation that new buildings of two or more storeys should have a lift, the LABC guidance note goes on to point out that there may be circumstances where a reduced standard is reasonable, specifically for small (e.g. with floor plates less than 100 sq m excluding stair core), low-rise buildings or buildings with low occupancy factors. All these factors are likely to apply to mixed-use street buildings, and so proposals for such buildings where a lift is not included are advised to state the reasons in the accompanying Access Statement.

In all cases, the minimum standard is provision of an ambulant disabled stair. Provision should also be made (for example, in the form of a floor cut-out) for future installation of a lift.

Building height is also affected by Part B of the Building Regulations 2010 (Fire) in relation to provision of alternative means of escape. Approved Document B (ADB, 2006 edition) advises that dwellings with floors above 7.5 m in height (usually three or more storeys) should either be provided with an alternative means of escape or fitted with a sprinkler. Similarly, small single-stair buildings with flats (e.g. close-grain street buildings) are affected by ADB2, which requires the top-floor level not to exceed 11 m above ground and there to be no more than three storeys above the ground-level storey (four storeys in total). Note that the equivalent height stipulated by Irish guidance (Technical Guidance Document B, 2006) is 7.5 m for dwelling houses but 10 m in most other instances. In mixed-use buildings with not more than three storeys above ground level, ADB2 suggests that the stairs may serve flats and other uses provided that the stairs are separated from each occupancy by protected lobbies. Fire-engineering approaches such as the use of detection and sprinkler systems may allow greater flexibility, particularly for open-plan townhouses.

While innovative design solutions may overcome regulatory constraints, buildings higher than five or six storeys begin to lose their sense of human scale, as contact with the ground is lost. This aspect of height was considered to be an important criterion in the setting of height limits in Vauban, Freiburg, where parents wanted to be able to summon their children from the upper floors.

Building depth and rear building set-back

The interrelationships between building depth and set-back and other factors, such as density, are described in Chapter 5, for a range of generic building footprints and different block and plot typologies. In general terms, the overall footprint of the building must be large enough to meet whatever space standards are applied to it (see also Chapter 5), while also providing sufficient space to both the front *and* rear to provide a satisfactory standard of amenity to its own occupants as well as to its neighbours. Achieving this balance lies at the heart of successful development management, not to mention neighbourly relations.

While it is convenient for designers and developers alike to avoid quantitative standards, it makes planning for plots more difficult because plot-based urbanism seeks to define a building envelope appropriate to a particular plot or plot typology without predetermining the building design. In other words, the plot needs to be configured to facilitate development that will be able to provide 'adequate' space, light and privacy, without determining the design or space-planning of the building *and* neighbouring buildings in advance. It cannot, therefore, rely on approaches to achieving privacy that depend on the design of all the neighbouring buildings being coordinated simultaneously so that, for example, opposing windows can be staggered or arranging compatible room types.

Rear building set-back and privacy

Most guidance, including the *London Housing Design Guide*, suggests that privacy should be 'adequate'. While it acknowledges that the conventional approach to separation distance (see Chapter 5) of 18 m to 21 m remains a useful yardstick, it states that this should not be rigidly applied. In contrast the older, yet still influential, *Essex Design Guide*, first published in 1973 and updated in 2005, suggests 25 m 'may' be acceptable, but some planning authorities may require more.[139]

Private (external) open space

In a similar vein, the *London Housing Design Guide* suggests a minimum standard of 5 sq m private open space for a two-person dwelling up to 9 sq m for a six-person dwelling, based on potential furniture and clothes-drying arrangements derived from the HCA's Housing Quality Indicators. The Code for Sustainable Homes does not give any numerical guidance but awards points on the premise that 'more is better'. This also contrasts starkly with the *Essex Design Guide*, which restates its preference for 100 sq m gardens for most houses (or at least 50 sq m per one- or two-bedroom house), and 25 sq m per flat where communal gardens are provided. Likewise, Supplementary Planning Guidance for housing in Northern Ireland suggests a minimum of 40 sq m and an average provision of at least 70 sq m, or 10 sq m to 30 sq m communal space per apartment, depending on occupancy.[140]

CABE's research strongly indicates that the provision of a generous private garden is a crucial factor for homebuyers choosing a home. CABE points out that demand for usable outdoor space is common to all life-stage groups; however, it is a particularly high priority for families with children. CABE also cites market studies testing attitudes to high density that showed strong resistance to smaller gardens.[141] More recent research carried out on behalf of the RIBA in 2010 found that outside space is the most important thing people look for when moving home (49%), together with room size (42%) and proximity to local services (42%).[142] Moreover, respondents did not believe that this is being provided by new private housing available on the market. Added to this, as shown in Chapter 5, the charge that the rear set-back distances implicit in providing more generous rear gardens prevents sustainable densities does not stand close scrutiny.

Thus, while it may be a moot point whether or not 5 sq m to 9 sq m is 'adequate' from the point of view of how the space is used, or indeed from the point of view of homebuyers' preferences, it is almost certain that the rear set-back distance produced by spaces this small will not be able to provide adequate sunlight, daylight or privacy between opposing windows.

Building depth and natural light

As a rule of thumb, the depth of all dual-aspect buildings is usually self-limiting to about 14 m because good daylighting from window walls cannot penetrate more than 6 m to 7 m.

Daylight is also affected by the proximity of neighbouring buildings, however. Thus, while the open space at the rear of the plot is usually assigned to amenity as residual space, the availability of both daylight and sunlight to the back of the building *and* the rear garden is affected by the proximity and height of the buildings around it. To complicate matters, the relationship between opposing windows must also be factored in, and also whether the amount and configuration of the space is appropriate to the occupancy of the dwelling.

Most quality standards discuss the need to provide 'adequate' sunlight and daylight, rear garden space and privacy, but contemporary guidelines and standards avoid setting quantitative standards for them. The interim *London Housing Design Guide* (2010), for example, requires only that direct sunlight will enter one habitable room for part of the day.

Guidance on site layout planning for daylight and sunlight published by the Building Research Establishment (BRE) states that, as a rule of thumb, a building will retain the potential for good interior diffuse daylighting provided that on all its faces no obstruction measured in a vertical section perpendicular to the main face, from a point 2 m above ground level, subtends an angle of more than 25° to the horizontal.[143]

The guidance goes on to recommend that no more than two fifths, and preferably no more than a quarter, of rear garden space should be prevented by buildings from receiving any sunlight at all on 21 March (equinox).

Applying both these rules of thumb together to notional south-facing rear gardens with opposing buildings of different height indicates that (for southern England and South Wales) rear separation distances of 12 m should be

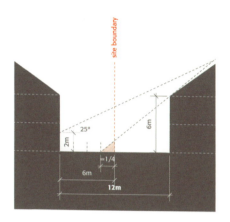

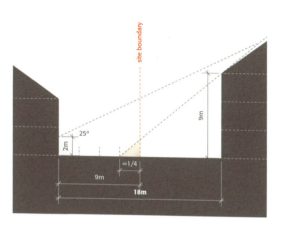

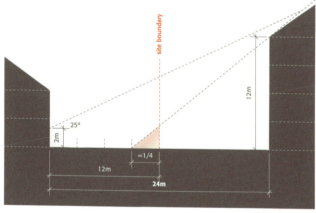

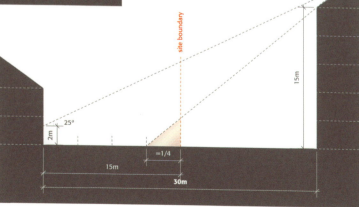

△ Indicative separation distances needed to meet BRE guidelines for daylight and overshadowing of rear gardens on 21 March for southern England and South Wales

satisfactory for two-storey buildings. This increases to 18 m for three-storey buildings, rising to 24 m for four-storey buildings and 30 m for five-storey buildings. This means that a distance-to-height ratio of 2:1 will generally result in adequate daylighting on the face of opposing buildings and solar access. Of course, the smaller one's garden space, the more valuable one quarter of it becomes and, conversely, the larger the garden, the less likely one quarter of it being in shadow is likely to matter to its occupants.

Other factors affecting set-back distances

Approved Document B (ADB1, 2006 edition) also provides guidance for dwellings affecting rear building set-back distances where escape from a basement is into an enclosed rear garden or courtyard. ADB1 states that for such an escape route to be acceptable the depth of the back garden should exceed the height of the house measured from ground level to the mid point of the back roof slope or exceed the height of any extension. In the case of a three-storey over basement house – a townhouse, for example – this could result in a rear set-back requirement of 10 m or more.

Taking into account the desirability of building in some tolerance allowing buildings to be extended backwards and/or upwards in the future, these considerations taken together would seem to validate applying conventional rear separation distances of between 18 m and 22 m to plot-based masterplanning for most townhouse typologies. Greater distances should be provided for where higher buildings, such as apartments or mixed-use buildings, are contemplated

Building width

The relationship of plot width to different building typologies, including row housing and attached mixed-use types, is discussed in some detail in Chapter 5. However, at the detailed level it is necessary to ensure that every individual plot in the casdastral masterplan will be viable for its intended purpose (i.e. building typology).

Consequently, plot subdivision boundaries must be much more precise than is expected (or necessary) in the case of most conventional masterplans, and the width of plot that is capable of accommodating the envisaged type of building must be calibrated against some known criteria: for example, the space standards with which it is expected to comply.

Where, for general masterplanning purposes, defining plots as x m or y m wide may be sufficient, it must be borne in mind that whatever dimension is specified assumes that the width of building required to meet any given space standards or room dimensions doesn't include the width of the external walls that enclose them. Defining plot width must therefore take account of the internal dimensions of the building, the width of party walls and, crucially, whether party walls will be constructed astride the plot boundary. Otherwise, tolerance must be 'built in' to allow party walls to be built within the plot. In terms of conventional party wall construction, guidance on Part E of the Building Regulations (ADE, 2003 edition, last updated 2010) limiting the passage of sound between separating walls includes examples showing how solid 215 mm brick or block wall construction with 13 mm lightweight plaster each side (241 mm in total) can meet the requirements. The reality of conventional building practices makes building to the millimetre unrealistic, however, suggesting that an easement of, say, 125 mm or 150 mm on each side of each shared boundary (giving a total width of 250 mm to 300 mm within which each party wall could be constructed) would provide adequate site tolerances.

For detached and semi-detached housing typologies, the building envelope must also define side boundary set-backs. Part B of the Building Regulations (ADB1) advises that external surfaces of walls of dwelling houses within 1 m of a boundary must meet Class 0 in respect of fire spread. In effect, this limits unprotected areas such as windows within 1 m of the side boundary. The acceptable unprotected area beyond 1 m is also constrained. For buildings other than dwelling houses (i.e. including flats), unprotected areas within 1 m are also subject to constraints detailed in ADB2.

The rules for developing house plots in Almere Poort stipulate a minimum distance of 2 m, and that any windows facing the side boundary must be fixed and opaque, unless otherwise formally agreed with the neighbour.

Detached and semi-detached houses are able to provide on-plot car-parking behind the building line, subject to the plot being sufficiently wide to accommodate the building and the car-parking space side by side. In this regard, it should be borne in mind that Lifetime Homes standards require the width of on-plot parking bays for dwelling houses to be capable of being expanded to 3.3 m for parking, which may have a knock-on effect on building footprint and overall plot width.

In Almere Poort, minimum plot widths of 4.5 m for row houses are set; wider plots may be purchased that increase in width in increments of 1.5 m. Similarly, two plots may be added together. In order to achieve close urban grain, however, it may be appropriate to also set a maximum plot width.

Boundary treatments

Variety in the design of boundary treatments, especially front garden fences, is somewhat less charming than variety in the design of buildings. Rules for building that stipulate a set-back from the street should consider what degree of control (if any) will be necessary or desirable to avoid a hotchpotch of different types and/or heights of fences. The building envelope should therefore prescribe whether boundary fences are required, or indeed permitted, and the heights of fences. It will be necessary to distinguish between fences separating front gardens, for example, and fences separating private gardens or access lanes at the rear, which may differ in height. It may also be appropriate to stipulate the width of entrances, taking into account whether the building type is intended to accommodate on-plot car-parking.

Stretching the building envelope

Rules, of course, are made to be broken, or at least stretched. The more continuous the street frontage generally, the less often gaps and blank walls occur between buildings, and the less likely they are to suffer from vandalism or neglect. Completely smooth building lines lack visual interest, however, and can funnel wind, generating uncomfortable microclimatic conditions. Fixing building heights or roof forms may also result in dull and monotonous streets.

Defining the building envelope as a range (or in terms of storey heights rather than in terms of dimensions) will tend to overcome this to a certain extent; however, the greatest scope for individual expression may flow from permitted deviations from the building envelope. Within the limits of the building envelope it may also be desirable to set minimum floor-to-ceiling heights, particularly for ground floors where it is hoped to encourage active uses. In combination with limits for overall building height, this can allow variety to occur naturally along the street.

Building lines may be varied to allow articulation and modelling of individual building façades, subject to avoiding the creation of 'dead' spaces at ground level that may collect wind-blown litter or attract anti-social behaviour. Horizontal projections and set-backs from the main building line, such as balconies, canopies, brise soleils, bays or oriel windows can also add interest without undermining a general sense of continuity and enclosure. The building envelope may also be broken by vertical projections such as chimneys, flues or antennae, which can add variety and interest to the roofscape. The building envelope may thus be used as a tool to define the limit of protrusions and recesses from the main building line(s) in three dimensions.

Making provision for mechanical plant is especially important to mixing commercial uses such as bars and restaurants with residential uses. In particular, extractors from kitchen areas must be properly ducted and discharged to avoid causing noise and smell nuisance to residents. The surest way to

Rijhuis

daklaag:
- vloeroppervlak max. 50%
van onderliggende laag
- dakvorm vrij

voorgevel daklaag:
- breedte max. 1/2 van
onderliggende gevel

bouwhoogte: max. 12 m.

voorgevel: min. 9 m.

uitbouw:
- max. 0,6 m buiten gevellijn
- min. 0,9 m uit gevel
- min. 3 m. boven trottoir

kavelbreedte:
veelvoud van 1,5 m.

insprong:
- 100% van gevelbreedte begane grond
- max 50% gevelbreedte van verdiepingen

bouwhoogte
achterbouwzone:
- max. 3 m. / 100%
bebouwing mogelijk

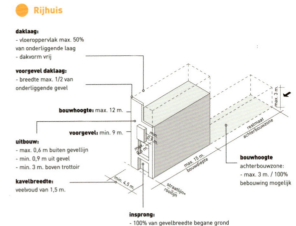

Stadspaleis

daklaag:
- vloeroppervlak max. 50%
van onderliggende laag
- dakvorm vrij

gevels daklaag:
breedte max. 1/3 van onderliggende gevel

erfscheiding perceel:
- haag
- hoogte: 2 m.

bouwhoogte: max. 13 m.
voorgevel: max. 10 m.

voorgevel: min. 6 m.

uitbouwen:
max. 1,2 m buiten gevellijn

bouwvolume:
minimum vereist

insprong:
- 100% van gevelbreedte
begane grond
- max 50% gevelbreedte
van verdiepingen

erfafscheiding straat:
haag 1 m.

parkeren:
-op eigen terrein via
inrit straat
-max. 2 inritten

verdiepingshoogte:
min. 20% vloeropp:
4 m. hoog (bruto)

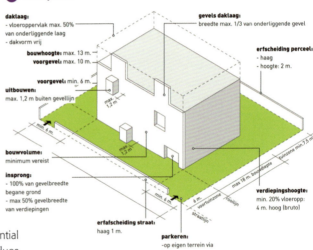

future-proof new mixed-use buildings against the potential for such conflicts is to require provision for ducting of flues to be made irrespective of the initial use, much in the same way that it is already common practice to require generous floor-to-ceiling heights at ground level. Where lift shafts are to be provided, for example, it makes sense to incorporate vertical risers for ducting alongside the lift enclosure, and to enable maintenance access to it to be obtained from the common areas above. ADB2 details guidance on provisions for protecting the shaft and ducting by compartment walls and by protecting the integrity of the ductwork respectively (note that using fire dampers to maintain the integrity of ducting from kitchens is not considered suitable because of the potential for build-up of grease within the duct, which can adversely affect the effectiveness of dampers). Floor-to-ceiling heights on the ground floor should be adequate to provide enough room for suspended ceilings to conceal horizontal runs if necessary, ensuring that the location of the vertical risers will not constrain future changes to the layout of the ground floor.

△ Building envelope rules for different residential typologies in part of Almere Poort: townhouse, detached house ('city palace'), canal house, flat and semi-detached house (Neutelings Riedijk Architects)

● Herenhuis

daklaag:
- vloeroppervlak max. 50%
van onderliggende laag
- dakvorm vrij

bouwhoogte: max. 16 m.

voorgevel daklaag:
breedte max. 1/2 van
onderliggende gevel

voorgevel: min. 12 m.

verdiepingshoogte:
beg. grond: min. 3,5 m

uitbouwen:
- max. 0,6 m buiten gevellijn
- min. 0,9 m uit gevel
- min. 3,5 m boven trottoir

kavelbreedte:
veelvoud van 1,5 m.

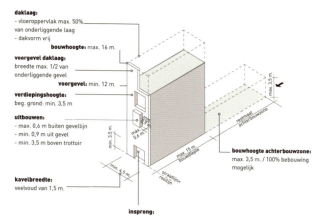

max. 3,5 m.

restmaat achterbouwzone

bouwhoogte achterbouwzone:
max. 3,5 m. / 100% bebouwing
mogelijk

max. 15 m. bouwdiepte

straatlijn= rooilijn

min. 4,5 m.

max. 0,6 m

min. 3,5 m.

insprong:
- 100% van gevelbreedte begane grond
- max 50% gevelbreedte van verdiepingen

● Flat

daklaag:
- vloeroppervlak max. 50% van
onderliggende laag
- dakvorm vrij

bouwhoogte: max. 24 m.

voorgevel daklaag:
setback voor en
achter min. 3 m.

voorgevel: 19,5 m.

verdiepingshoogte:
beg. grond: min. 4,5 m.

uitbouw:
- max. 0,6 m. buiten
gevellijn
- min. 0,9 m. uit gevel
- min. 4,5 m. boven
trottoir

kavelbreedte:
veelvoud van 1,5 m.

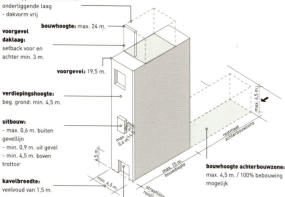

max. 4,5 m.

restmaat achterbouwzone

bouwhoogte achterbouwzone:
max. 4,5 m. / 100% bebouwing
mogelijk

max. 15 m. bouwdiepte

straatlijn= rooilijn

min. 4,5 m.

max. 0,6 m

4,5 m.

insprong:
- 100% van gevelbreedte begane grond
- max 50% gevelbreedte van verdiepingen

● Twee- onder- een- kap

breedte max. 1/3 van onderliggende gevel

daklaag:
- vloeroppervlak max. 50%
van onderliggende laag
- dakvorm vrij

bouwhoogte: max. 13 m.

voorgevel: max. 10 m.

voorgevel: min. 6 m.

uitbouwen:
max. 1,2 m. buiten gevellijn

vaste inrit:
- breedte: max 3 m.
- parkeren op eigen
terrein via inrit straat.

bouwvolume:
minimum vereist

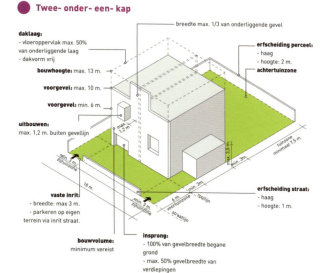

erfscheiding perceel:
- haag
- hoogte: 2 m.

achtertuinzone

max. 3,5 m.

tuinzone minimaal 7,5 m.

min. 3m.

min. m. zijtuinzone

18 m.

max. 1,2 m

min. 3 m. zijtuinzone

6 m. voortuinzone

straatlijn

rooilijn

erfscheiding straat:
- haag
- hoogte: 1 m.

insprong:
- 100% van gevelbreedte begane
grond
- max. 50% gevelbreedte van
verdiepingen

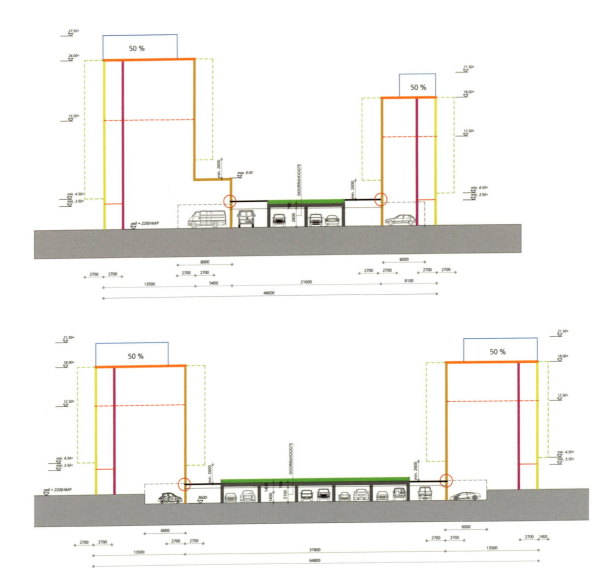

△ Building envelope rules for typical
close-grain mixed-use blocks in
Homeruskwartier Centrum, Almere
Poort, the Netherlands

The building line may also be penetrated by vehicular and/or pedestrian entrances into the interior of the block or plot. In general terms, while such variations may add welcome relief to the continuity of the building line, they need to avoid causing obstructions at street level or potentially impeding access by emergency services.

6.3   RULES FOR COORDINATION

One of the most attractive features of close-grain and mixed-grain streets is that all the buildings are potentially different. Individual street buildings or townhouses may be built at different times, or recycled, or built at the same time but designed by different architects. This requires a degree of coordination.

Approaches to coordination of adjoining plots can be 'hands on' or 'hands off'.

6.3.1 Coordinating party walls

Contiguous buildings, by definition, share boundaries. Although it is possible for flanking walls to abut each other, this is wasteful of space, materials and construction costs. The need to coordinate party walls arises from their construction either on one side or other of the property boundary or, preferably, straddling the boundary, and how the construction and costs of those and any other shared elements are apportioned, particularly when development on one side precedes that on the other.

The construction of party walls in England and Wales is governed by the Party Wall etc. Act 1996. Under the Act, a new party wall may only be built astride the boundary with the agreement of the adjoining owner. The agreement, drafted by a party wall surveyor, may provide for costs to be shared between the owners where the benefits and use of the wall are also shared. If an agreement isn't made, however, the wall can only be built within the boundary, and at the expense of the owner. Footings may be placed under the

adjoining owner's land, but this doesn't extend to reinforced concrete, which requires consent from the adjoining owner. The Act also grants rights to enter the land to carry out works that are necessary pursuant to the Act (subject to giving appropriate notice etc., as stipulated in the Act).[144]

The Party Wall etc. Act is also relevant to construction adjacent to the boundary if excavation/construction of foundations is within 3 m and lower down than the adjoining owner's foundations, or within 6 m if the work cuts a line drawn downwards at 45° from the bottom of the adjoining owner's foundations.

In contrast to the tightly prescribed legislative framework for party walls operating in England and Wales (no such legislation exists in Ireland), the rules for development stipulated by the municipality of Almere merely point out that it is in the interests of both parties to share the costs of foundations and the like, and that it is beneficial to communicate regularly in respect of elements such as drain pipes that may affect one another. More specifically, they require party walls to be built in such a way that a connection between adjoining buildings can be made, and that party walls that will be exposed pending the construction of the neighbouring building (i.e. that aren't designed to be permanently exposed) are properly insulated.

In order to address the issues surrounding the need for consent between adjoining owners being required to build astride the plot boundaries, contiguous plots could alternatively be leased or sold subject to easements along the length of the shared boundaries. The effect of this would be to permit the construction of party walls and associated footings straddling the boundary, which would be in the interests of both parties. The physical limits of the party walls would be set by the rules for building – the building envelope – and granted as easements with the sale of the plot. This would obviate the need to go through lengthy party wall procedures to determine whether both parties consent to a shared party wall, thus avoiding two sets of walls being built, one on each side of the divide. Details relating to flashing, insulation and so on can then be agreed through normal party wall procedures, where necessary.

Where one building proceeds in advance of its future neighbour(s), this avoids the potential waste of space associated with building the party walls entirely within the plot, but doesn't provide a mechanism for sharing the cost. The first to build would therefore incur greater cost than the neighbours on either side, even though they also benefit from the use of the party wall.

In this context, it is common practice in northern Europe to engage a separate designer or supervisor specifically tasked with ensuring that constituent plots making up the block in his or her charge are properly coordinated. Where a building cooperative is formed, the employment of a shared building contractor also eases coordination and helps to obtain economies of scale.

An intermediate approach is for a single developer, the landowner, to put in place a ground floor or basement slab with rising party walls and service connections, and then to sell on plots individually or collectively subject to party wall agreements being reached, and appointing a site management coordinator. Prospective developers of individual plots can then agree, depending on the structural loads imposed by their respective designs, on the apportionment of costs.

This approach has been proposed by developers Urban Splash for 26 townhouse plots for sale in New Islington, Manchester. The development, known as 'Tutti Frutti', comprises a row of contiguous 'small' (4 m wide × 15 m deep), 'medium' (4.5 m wide × 15 m deep) and 'large' (5 m wide × 15 m deep) plots for sale with a 250-year leasehold. Urban Splash organised a competition for interested parties to submit designs following some simple 'rules':

- ☐ one house per plot
- ☐ no part of the building to project beyond the plot boundary
- ☐ ventilated bin store complying with the local authority's collection regime (on plot)
- ☐ all houses to meet Code for Sustainable Homes level 3
- ☐ compliance with the local authority's access standards
- ☐ submission of applications for planning permission in groups of six or eight.

The developer committed to employing a structural engineer to coordinate this. They were responsible for designing the party walls for each house based on wall loading criteria supplied by each participant, and were to construct the walls up to 900 mm in height. Plots would thus be taken over with the slab and rising walls in place as well as service connections.

Thereafter the developer agreed to employ a party wall surveyor for consultation purposes, and fixed rates for party wall construction agreed with each party's builder. The walls were to be constructed at the same time as the dwellings, with contracts agreed on the basis that the first person to start construction would pay for the party walls as per the agreed rates, and then recoup the monies from the neighbour within a set period of time. Costs were to be apportioned proportionately by the party wall surveyor, depending on the load imposed by each side.

Waterproofing details at party wall junctions were also to be agreed through the party wall surveyor, with warranties from the designer/contractor to the benefit of the houses on each side of the wall.

Lastly, the developer undertook to employ both a site coordination manager and construction design and management (CDM) coordinator to ease coordination between the different stages of work being undertaken by different builders on site and to comply with health and safety requirements respectively. Unfortunately, the high degree of interest expressed in the scheme was overtaken by recession, and development stalled. A planning application for a larger, more conventional scheme (albeit with customisable elements) has since been submitted.[145]

6.3.2 Coordinating the interface between private and shared elements

As outlined in Chapter 5, some block types rely on the juxtaposition of private plots with shared facilities, typically shared courtyards or shared parking courts. In the case of podium blocks, where the shared amenity space is located above a car park, the junction between buildings and the deck must be coordinated to ensure that some consistency in finish and appearance is achieved, that structural loads are agreed and that critical junctions meet criteria limiting the spread of fire between them. Again, a distinction needs to be drawn between elements of the block in which it is desirable or intended to generate variety – namely the buildings – and shared elements such as footpaths, where consistency is necessary to ensure that materials are compatible and that building regulations concerning things like trip hazards and navigation by visually impaired people are met.

Where shared elements are an integral part of the block, the most straightforward way to ensure coordination is make it the responsibility of a single designer. In the case of close-grain mixed-use plots being developed in Almere Poort, this is achieved through cooperation between the members of building cooperatives, whose individual plots also buy a share in the communal space. In Sweden, a single coordinating architect is also tasked with the design of shared elements and how they fit together.

On a technical level, it would appear likely that the introduction of building information modelling (BIM) software may significantly improve the potential for error-free coordination of multiple designers in the same space compared to conventional 2D CAD systems.

6.3.3 Coordinating ancillary uses

The rules for building also need to define how the building will function in use, particularly in relation to aspects that don't necessarily have a predetermined spatial expression. In the case of residential plots this will include:

- [ ] how much of the building can be used for home-based employment (or live-work)
- [ ] requirements for on-plot parking
- [ ] requirements for bicycle parking.

For mixed-use buildings, a greater range of requirements may need to be specified:

- [ ] how much floor area can be used for commercial purposes (e.g. shops)
- [ ] requirements for storage of commercial waste
- [ ] provision for signage or outdoor seating
- [ ] provision for vertical service risers
- [ ] provision for fixing utilities to the street façade etc.

As the future uses may not be known when the masterplan is made, uses generating unusually high demand for parking or visitor numbers may also be required to justify their provision.

6.4 BRINGING IT ALL TOGETHER

The rules for building and the rules for coordination between buildings can be brought together as part of the overall cadastral masterplan document, or appended to it as a suite of supporting documents. In order to account for the unique features pertaining to each individual plot, however, an additional layer of plot-specific detail is required to overcome the vagaries of topography and other variables that make it impossible to guarantee that every plot will conform to type in every way, shape or form.

Thus, while the generic building envelope pertaining to a particular building type, such as a townhouse or a mixed-use street building, can be described in diagrammatic form as part of the cadastral masterplan, plot-specific detail is necessary to take account of and to record variations between plots of the same type. These variations may arise, for example, where one block is completely orthogonal but another is deformed. This may cause some plots to be irregularly shaped or introduce variation in size. Other plot-specific factors such as easements for public services may also need to be recorded.

Plot-based masterplans in the Netherlands thus tie the sale of each plot to individual *plot-specific* documents that form part of the contract of sale. These documents, known as *kavel passports* (plot passports):

- ☐ cross-reference the plot with its location on the cadastral masterplan
- ☐ define the building typology that is permitted
- ☐ set out the metes and bounds of the plot in diagrammatic form in relation to the public realm
- ☐ list the rules for building (the building envelope, permitted heights, etc.)
- ☐ state the rules for coordinating between adjoining buildings, where relevant
- ☐ define key terms such as building height, ground level, etc.
- ☐ set out the role of the project supervisor, who has discretion to arbitrate on the minor deviations from the rules that are considered to be in harmony with the intent and spirit of the scheme.

◁ Visualisation of close-grain mixed-use
  blocks, Almere Poort, the Netherlands

△ Recently completed townhouses in
  Almere Poort

7 Conclusion

Close-grain plots are a character-giving feature of successful streets, villages and town centres. They impart character by generating a diversity of architectural forms that can support locally based economies, social networks and a wide range of compatible uses in close proximity to each other. Plots are self-contained units of landholding. The small-scale nature of the buildings and uses they support means that each is able to adapt and change without disrupting the others. As a result, they are jointly and severally adaptable to changing fortunes, they make efficient use of land and resources, and produce compact building forms that can reduce heat loss and the damaging effects of this on the environment.

The current UK government's promise to make it easier for people to build their own homes, together with the growing consensus that mixed uses and mixed-tenure housing are vital components of sustainable communities, also has the potential to dovetail with the government's localism agenda. Significant planning powers will be devolved to Neighbourhoods in England, for example, and these powers offer the potential for communities to engage in plot-based approaches to development at a scale that is more appropriate to their locality. Where Neighbourhood Development Orders (NDOs) are deployed, for example, they may be able to do this without having to apply for planning permission. Where normal development management procedures are relaxed, alternative safeguards need to be put in place.

Carefully planned and integrated as part of an overall urban, landscape and movement framework or masterplan, plots offer a coherent way of achieving diversity, balanced urban densities and more environmentally, economically and socially sustainable places. Projects in European countries – such as Tübingen Südstadt and Vauban in Germany, Ijburg and Almere Poort in the Netherlands, among others – have shown that plot-based urbanism can generate vibrant new neighbourhoods and new town centres with a high degree of diversity – variety, mixed uses and tenure, social inclusion – and, most of all, a quality and sense of place, from which

we in the UK and Ireland have a lot to learn. One of the lessons gleaned from these experiments is that architects and urban designers have a vital role to play in providing leadership and helping their clients and other stakeholders to realise their vision through creative design solutions.

Implementing plot-based development in the UK and Ireland is less straightforward than conventional modes of development, because it relies on forward funding of infrastructure in order for serviced plots to be sold on, as well as participation by a greater number and variety of stakeholders in the development process. The potential benefits are significant. It opens the development market to a larger number of different developers and designers operating at different scales, and it opens up the potential for collaboration between end-users. Cutting out the 'middle-man' – the volume developer – in this way can reap significant savings for self builders, for example, but the wider social benefit associated with building a community is itself a worthy goal. Case examples suggest that this is likely to be easier where public ownership of development land can be secured; however, there are already solid precedents for private developers taking a more 'enlightened' and longer-term approach to their investment, and promoting serviced plots as part of their offer.

A range of measures that could be introduced to facilitate plot-based urbanism have been identified. They focus on forward funding of infrastructure, enabling and regulatory measures, and alternative development models. Initiatives that can be used to forward-fund infrastructure include the Community Infrastructure Levy (CIL), which has already been introduced, tax increment financing (TIF), which is currently being introduced, land value taxation (LVT) and reform of value added taxation (VAT), both of which are recurring political issues. Other initiatives fall into the category of enabling and/or regulatory measures. These include more extensive use of existing planning powers such as Local Development Orders (LDOs) and Neighbourhood Development Orders (NDOs), alongside design codes. In terms of regulation, there is a strong argument that current planning controls do not provide adequate protection to historic patterns of plot subdivision and do not give adequate scope for proposals that involve the amalgamation of contiguous plots to be considered. This is compounding the loss of diversity from existing traditional streets.

Alternative development models promote plot-based urbanism indirectly as a means of regulating the supply of land to stabilise the market and maximise uplift through the masterplanning process. On the demand side, there seems to be an as yet untapped latent demand for self building fuelled by the popularity of TV programmes such as *Grand Designs*, but representative organisations like the National Self Build Association (NaSBA) claim that this demand is being thwarted by a lack of serviced plots in suitable locations. Plot-based developments already exist in the UK, but they have sprung up sporadically *despite* the status quo rather than because of it.

Of course, changing the regulatory and taxation regimes affecting development lies outside the gift of everyday practising urban designers, architects and planners. Nevertheless, it is eminently possible to achieve the benefits of plot-based urbanism within the current regimes. This is already happening on a small scale throughout the UK.

In order for plot-based urbanism to work, however, it needs to reconcile the divergent agendas of conventional masterplanning with more incremental development approaches. Contemporary urban design theory and urban design guidance wax lyrical about the qualities of places that appear to have grown organically over time, but this rather nostalgic view jars with the reality of prevailing urban design practice, which favours comprehensive masterplanning and comprehensive development. But whereas comprehensive design and development tend to produce dull and soulless places lacking real character, ad hoc design and development that is allowed to occur on a plot-by-plot basis is more likely to produce places that are fragmented and chaotic.

This book argues that the benefits of both approaches can be reconciled by introducing the cadastral masterplan. This approach advances conventional masterplanning, which tends to focus on the larger urban structure of blocks and streets, by designing the subdivision of its constituent blocks into discrete plots. What is, perhaps, more radical is the implication this has for urban form and procurement, because it opens up the possibility of individual plots or groups of plots being sold on to, and also designed and developed by, *individuals* or groups of individuals.

The principal strategic approaches to ensuring greater diversity of urban forms include allocating individual blocks to different developers, allocating *parts* of individual blocks to different developers, and allocating individual plots *within* blocks to different developers. Hybrids of these approaches are also possible.

Superficially, at least, the laying out of blocks and plots for development is a simple matter. Simply defined, plots are two-dimensional shapes that define property boundaries. Blocks are clusters of plots occupied by buildings that define territory, separated from each other by shared movement networks, or streets. Blocks may comprise a single landholding or be subdivided into two or more plots. But this simplicity is deceptive. Not only is it imperative that plots are configured together to make urban blocks that will contribute to a compact and permeable urban structure: they must also be primed to receive the desired type, use and size of building. The design and use of the buildings that will occupy the plots may not be known when the plots are laid out or sold, so their configuration must be robust enough for the buildings themselves to meet a plethora of regulations and standards. In other words, although no detail is required to lay out plots, all the detail must be anticipated.

A number of different approaches to combining close-grain and mixed-grain plot and building typologies are possible. The illustrated examples in this book show the principal block and plot options appropriate to the European context, but they are not exhaustive. The potential for variation is extensive, but experience combined with best practice guidance suggests that tried and tested building typologies such as townhouses, street buildings with vertical mixed uses, and mixed-use apartment buildings arranged in perimeter block formats, are the most robust and adaptable forms, and so are likely to produce the best results.

A wide range of issues need to be considered in the configuration of blocks and the subdivision of blocks into plots at the masterplanning stage. It is important to stress at the outset that plot-based urbanism does not entail the wholesale roll-out of close-grain plots. A mixed grain of large and small plots is likely to be appropriate and, in some cases, necessary to produce sustainable densities and to provide variety and choice of building types, land uses and tenures in the right locations. Likewise, it will not be viable for every plot or street to incorporate mixed uses. The appropriate location and distribution of uses and density is intimately connected to accessibility criteria and population catchments.

Each plot and building type has its own advantages and disadvantages; each has different implications for density and the degree or type of diversity of form that it is likely to produce. As a result, each is more or less suited to differing urban contexts and different uses or combinations of uses, whether urban, peri-urban or suburban.

One of the key challenges is to reconcile policy aspirations promoting higher density development with negative perceptions of high-density living and the allied demand for lower-scaled, 'own front door' developments with front and rear gardens. This is especially important if families with children are to be tempted back from the suburbs. The illustrative examples demonstrate that traditional building typologies such as the townhouse, mixed-use street buildings and mansion house typologies are capable of being adapted to modern needs. They can meet demand for private garden space and they can also produce sustainable mid-range densities.

Once a cadastral masterplan of plots is determined, the actual logistics of coordinating a wide variety of actors in the delivery of infrastructure, procurement and construction on adjacent plots – 'cheek by jowl', as it were – presents many challenges. Parameters that need to be defined to regulate plot-based development have been explored, including detailed standards and regulations affecting the design of buildings that influence the definition of the building envelope, and how building 'on the ground' may be coordinated. All of these factors need to be weighed against each other to balance the need for clear guidance with individual expression. A tried and tested way of doing this is design coding. Design codes in the UK have been criticised for stifling diversity of architectural form whereas their European counterparts have been praised for stimulating it. The critical difference between these codes is that the UK ones, to date, have neglected the significance of the plot. Experience of places where plot-based urbanism has been prioritised, notably Germany, Sweden, France and the Netherlands, illustrates the continued relevance of design codes to regulating building form within defined spatial parameters, but without constraining architectural freedom of expression.

There is no reason why the success of these projects can't be replicated – and improved upon – elsewhere. First, the value of plots must be appreciated and existing historical plot subdivisions protected. Second, the plot must be reinvented to meet modern needs and expectations, and third, policy must be reformulated to provide explicit support for plot-based urbanism. Above all, the plot must be reintroduced to the development mix. To paraphrase the motto adopted by the citizen's forum in Vauban, Freiburg, which is an exemplary model of what sustainable plot-based urbanism can achieve: 'we can re-make the world as we want it'.

▷ **Townhouses under construction in Almere Poort**

references

Alexander, C., Ishikawa, S. and Silverstein, M., 1977. *A Pattern Language: Towns, buildings, construction*. Oxford University Press: New York.

Alexander, C., Neis, H., Anninou, A. and King, I., 1987. *A New Theory of Urban Design*. Oxford University Press: Oxford.

Barton, H., Grant, M. and Guise, R., 2010. *Shaping Neighbourhoods for Local Health and Global Sustainability* (2nd edition). Routledge: Abingdon.

Bürklin, T. and Peterek, M., 2008. *Urban Building Blocks*. Birkhäuser: Basel.

CABE, 2004. *Creating Successful Masterplans*. CABE: London.

CABE, 2004. *Housing Audit: Assessing the design quality of new homes, London, the South East and East of England*. CABE: London

CABE, 2005. *What Home Buyers Want: Attitudes and decision making among consumers*. CABE: London.

CABE, undated. *The Use of Urban Design Codes: Building sustainable communities*. CABE: London.

Campbell, K., 2011. *Massive Small: The operating programme for smart urbanism*. Urban Exchange: London.

Collins, J. and Moren, P., 2009. *Good Practice Guide: Negotiating the Planning Maze* (3rd edition). RIBA Publishing: London.

Congress for the New Urbanism. Charter of the Congress for the New Urbanism, 1996. In: Nicolaides, B.M. and Wiese, A. (eds), 2006. *The Suburb Reader*. Routledge: New York.

Congress for the New Urbanism, 2004. *Charter of the New Urbanism*. McGraw-Hill: New York.

Conzen, M. R. G., Morphogenesis and Structure of the Historic Townscape in Britain. In: Conzen, M. P. (ed.), 2004. *M.R.G. Conzen: Thinking about Urban Form. Papers on urban morphology, 1932–1998*. Peter Lang: Bern.

Cousins, M., 2009. *Design Quality in New Housing: Learning from the Netherlands*. Taylor and Francis: Abingdon.

Cowan, R., 2005. *The Dictionary of Urbanism*. Streetwise Press: Tisbury.

Cullen, G., 1961. *Townscape*. Architectural Press: London.

Cullingworth, B. and Nadin, V., 2006. *Town Planning in the UK* (14th edition). Routledge: Abingdon.

Department for Communities and Local Government, 2002. *Mixed-use Development, Practice and Potential*. Available at www.communities.gov.uk.

Department for Communities and Local Government, 2002. *The Party Wall etc. Act 1996: An explanatory booklet*. CLG: London.

Department for Communities and Local Government, 2006. *Preparing Design Codes: A practice manual*. CLG: London.

Department for Communities and Local Government, 2010. *Code for Sustainable Homes: Technical guide*. CLG: London. Available at: www.planningportal.gov.uk/uploads/code_for_sustainable_homes_techguide.pdf

Department for Communities and Local Government, January 2010. *Garden Developments: Understanding the issues – an investigation into residential development on gardens in England*. CLG: London.

Department for Communities and Local Government, June 2010. *Planning Policy Statement 3: Housing*. CLG: London.

Department for Communities and Local Government, May 2011. *The Community Infrastructure Levy: An overview*. CLG: London.

Department for Communities and Local Government, July 2011. *Draft National Planning Policy Framework*. CLG: London.

Department for Communities and Local Government, November 2011. *Laying the foundations: A Housing Strategy for England*. HM Government: London.

Department for Communities and Local Government, March 2012. *National Planning Policy Framework*. CLG: London.

Department of the Environment (NI), 1998. *Planning Policy Statement 1: General Principles*. Department of the Environment: Belfast.

Department of Environment, Heritage and Local Government, 2007. *Sustainable Urban Housing Design Standards for New Apartments: Guidelines for planning authorities*. Government of Ireland: Dublin.

Department of Environment, Heritage and Local Government, 2009. *Guidelines for Planning Authorities on Sustainable Residential Development in Urban Areas (Cities, Towns and Villages)*. Government of Ireland: Dublin. Available at: http://www.environ.ie/en/Publications/DevelopmentandHousing/Planning/FileDownLoad,19164,en.pdf

Department of the Environment, Transport and the Regions, 1998. *Places, Streets and Movement*. DETR: London.

Department of the Environment, Transport and the Regions, 1998. *The Use of Density in Urban Planning*. DETR: London.

Department of the Environment, Transport and the Regions, 2000. *By Design: Urban design in the planning system – towards better practice*. DETR: London.

Department for Transport, 2007. *Manual for Streets*. Thomas Telford Publishing: London.

Duddy, C., 2001. The Western Suburb of Medieval Dublin: Its first century. *Irish Geography*, 34(2), pp. 157–175.

Dunham-Jones, E. and Williamson, J., 2009. *Retrofitting Suburbia: Urban design solutions for redesigning suburbs*. John Wiley and Sons: New Jersey.

English Partnerships and the Housing Corporation, 2000. *Urban Design Compendium*. English Partnerships: London.

Essex County Council, 2005. *Essex Design Guide*. Available at: http://www.the-edi.co.uk/downloads/19715_essexdesignguide.pdf

Falk, N., 2010. *How the Dutch fund infrastructure: Lessons from Vathorst in Amersfoort*. Urbed (unpublished).

Falk, N. and Munday, B., 2010. Forgotton Suburbs and Smarter Growth. *Urban Design*, 115, pp. 23–25.

Frampton, K., 1992. *Modern Architecture: A critical history* (3rd edition). Thames and Hudson: London.

Gehl, J., 2001. *Life Between Buildings*. Arkitektens Forlag: Skive.

Gemeente Almere, 2010. *Homeruskwartier Centrum: Zelf Bouwen*. Municipality of Almere. Available at: http://www.homeruskwartier-centrum.nl/

Greater London Authority, 2011. *The London Plan: Spatial Development Strategy for Greater London, July 2011*. GLA: London.

Greater London Council, 1977. *GLC Preferred Dwelling Plans*. Architectural Press: London.

HATC, 2006. *Housing Space Standards*. Greater London Authority: London.

Hertzberger, H., 2005. *Lessons for Students in Architecture*. Translated from Dutch by Rike, I., 2005. 010 Publications: Rotterdam.

Howard, E., 1902. Garden Cities of Tomorrow. In: Nicolaides, B.M. and Wiese, A. (eds), 2006. *The Suburb Reader*. Routledge: New York.

Imrie, R., 2006. *Accessible Housing: Quality, disability and design*. Routledge: London.

Imrie, R. and Street, E., 2011. *Architectural Design and Regulation*. Wiley-Blackwell: Chichester.

Jacobs, J., 1961. *The Death and Life of Great American Cities*. Penguin Books: London.

Jones, P., Roberts M. and Morris, L., 2007. *Rediscovering Mixed-Use Streets: The contribution of local high streets to sustainable communities*. The Policy Press: Bristol.

Klettner, A., 15 December 2010. *Riba urges architects to get involved with localism*. Available at: http://m.bdonline.co.uk/news/riba-urges-architects-to-get-involved-with-localism/5010411.article

Kostof, S., 1991. *The City Shaped: Urban patterns and meanings through history*. Thames and Hudson: London.

Le Corbusier, 1973. *The Athens Charter*. Grossman Publishers: New York.

Levitt, D., 2010. *The Housing Design Handbook: A guide to good practice*. Routledge: Oxford.

Lilley, K. D., 2001. Urban Planning and the Design of Towns in the Middle Ages: The Earls of Devon and their 'New Towns'. *Planning Perspectives*, 16, pp. 1–24.

Littlefair, P. J., 1991. *Site Layout Planning for Sunlight and Daylight: A guide to good practice*. Building Research Establishment: Watford.

Local Government Group and the Planning Advisory Service, 2011. *LDOs and Localism: Can Local Development Orders contribute to the new planning agenda?* Local Government Group: London.

Logan, K., 2010. Sustainable Suburbia. *Urban Design*, 115, pp. 29–30.

London Development Agency, 2010. *London Housing Design Guide (interim edition)*. LDA: London. Available at: http://www.designforlondon.gov.uk/uploads/media/Interim_London_Housing_Design_Guide.pdf

Marshall, S. (ed.), 2011. *Urban Coding and Planning*. Routledge: Abingdon.

McCullogh, N., 2007. *Dublin: An urban history – the plan of the city*. Anne Street Press in association with the Lilliput Press: Dublin.

Mitchell, C., 2010. Building a New Suburbia. *Urban Design*, 115, pp. 26–28.

National Planning Policy Framework Practitioners Advisory Group, 2011. Available at: http://www.nppfpractitionersadvisorygroup.org/wp-content/uploads/2011/05/A-proposed-draft-from-the-Practitioners-Advisory-Group.pdf

National Self Build Association, 2008. *Self Build as a Volume Housing Solution*. NaSBA.

NEF (New Economics Foundation), 2010. *Re-imagining the High Street: Escape from clone town Britain*. NEF: London.

Nicolaides, B. M. and Wiese, A. (eds), 2006. *The Suburb Reader*. Routledge: New York.

Office of the Deputy Prime Minister, 2004. *Safer Places: The planning system and crime prevention*. OPDM: London. Available at http://www.securedbydesign.com/pdfs/safer_places.pdf

Office of the Deputy Prime Minister, 2005. *Planning Policy Statement 1: Delivering Sustainable Development*.

Owen, S. (Department for Communities and Local Government), 2011. *Lessons from International Self Build Housing Practices*. Prepared for the National Self Build Association (NaSBA) on behalf of the joint Government-Industry Self Build Working Group. Available at: www.nasba.org.uk/Content/Reports.aspx

Palin, J. J., 1995. *The Suburbs*. McGraw-Hill: New York.

Panerai, P., Castex, J., Depaule, J. C. and Samuels, I., 2004. *Urban Forms: The death and life of the urban block*. Architectural Press: Oxford.

PlacesMatter!, 2009. *The Economic Value of Good Design*. PlacesMatter! and the Northwest Regional Development Agency: Liverpool.

Portas, M., 2011. *The Portas Review: An independent review into the future of our high streets*. Department for Business, Innovation and Skills: London.

Res Publica, 2011. *The Right to Retail: Can localism save Britain's small retailers?*

Ritchie, A. and Thomas, R. (eds), 2009. *Sustainable Urban Design: An environmental approach* (2nd edition). London and New York: Taylor and Francis.

Roberts, M. and Greed, C., 2001. *Approaching Urban Design*. Longman: Harlow.

Rowe, C. and Koetter, F., 1978. *Collage City*. MIT Press: Cambridge.

Royal Institute of British Architects, 2010. *The Case for Space: The size of England's new homes*. RIBA: London.

Savills Research, 2010. *Development Layout: Finding a solution to urban development and regeneration by building the modern residential city*. Available at http://pdf.euro.savills.co.uk/spotlight-on/spotlight-on-development-layout.pdf.

Savills Research, 2010. *Market in Minutes: UK residential development land*. Available at: http://pdf.euro.savills.co.uk/uk/market-in-minute-reports/residential-development-land--oct-2010.pdf.

Scottish Government, 2008. *Planning Advice Note 83: Masterplanning*. Available at: http://www.scotland.gov.uk/Resource/Doc/244134/0068213.pdf

Scottish Government, 2010. *Scottish Planning Policy*. Available at: http://www.scotland.gov.uk/Publications/2010/02/03132605/0

Scottish Government, 2011. *Delivering Better Places in Scotland: A guide to learning from broader experience*. Available at: http://www.scotland.gov.uk/Publications/2010/12/31110906/0

Smith, A., 1776. *An Inquiry into the Nature and Causes of the Wealth of Nations* (fifth edition). Harriman House: Hampshire.

Talen, E., 2006. Design for Diversity: Evaluating the context of socially mixed neighbourhoods. *Journal of Urban Design*, 11(1), pp. 1–32.

Talen, E., 2008. *Design for Diversity: Exploring socially mixed neighbourhoods*. Oxford: Architectural Press.

The Heritage Council and Dublin City Council, 2004. *Built to Last: The sustainable reuse of buildings*. The Heritage Council and Dublin City Council: Dublin.

Urban Task Force, 1999. *Towards an Urban Renaissance: Final Report of the Urban Task Force*. Department of the Environment, Transport and the Regions. E & FN Spon: London.

Vitruvius, M., date unknown. *The Ten Books on Architecture*. Translated by Morgan, M., H. and Howard, A. A., 1960. Dover Press: New York.

Welsh Assembly Government, 2009. *Planning Policy Wales Technical Advice Note 12: Design*. Available at: http://wales.gov.uk/docs/desh/publications/090807tan12en.pdf

Welsh Assembly Government, 2011. *Planning Policy Wales* (edition 4). Available at: http://wales.gov.uk/docs/desh/publications/110228ppwedition4en.pdf

Whitehand, J. W. R., 1987. *The Changing Face of Cities: A study of development cycles and urban form*. Basil Blackwell: Oxford.

Whitehand, J. W. R., 1992. *The Making of the Urban Landscape*. Basil Blackwell: Oxford.

Whitelaw, I., 2007. *A Measure of all Things: The story of measurement through the ages*. David and Charles: Hove.

endnotes

1 See, for example, CABE, *Housing Audits: Assessing the design quality of new homes*. CABE: London, 2004–06, which concluded that up to one third of schemes assessed should not have received planning permission.

2 English Partnerships and the Housing Corporation, *Urban Design Compendium*. English Partnerships: London, 2000, p. 4.

3 Department of the Environment, Transport and the Regions and the Commission for Architecture and the Built Environment, *By Design: Urban design in the planning system: towards better practice*, 2000, p. 14.

4 CABE, *Creating Successful Masterplans*. CABE: London, 2004.

5 See for example:

   English Partnerships and the Housing Corporation, 2000, *op. cit.*

   Department for Communities and Local Government. *Mixed-use Development, Practice and Potential*, 2002. Available at www.communities.gov.uk.

   Jones, P., Roberts M. and Morris, L., *Rediscovering Mixed-Use Streets: The contribution of local high streets to sustainable communities*. The Policy Press: Bristol, 2007.

   NEF (New Economics Foundation), *Re-imagining the High Street: Escape from clone town Britain*. NEF: London, 2010.

   Res Publica, *The Right to Retail: Can localism save Britain's small retailers?* 2011.

6 Department for Communities and Local Government, 2002, *op. cit.*

7 Jones, P., Roberts M. and Morris, L., 2007, *op. cit.*

8 English Partnerships and the Housing Corporation, 2000, *op cit.*, p. 12.

9 Jones, P., Roberts M. and Morris, L., 2007, *op. cit.*, p. xii.

10 Jacobs, J., *The Death and Life of Great American Cities*. New York: Vintage Books, 1961, pp. 164–165.

11 Talen, E., *Design for Diversity: Exploring socially mixed neighbourhoods*. Oxford: Architectural Press, 2008, p. 38.

12   Urban Task Force, *Towards an Urban Renaissance: Final report of the Urban Task Force*. Department of the Environment, Transport and the Regions. E & FN Spon: London, 1999, p. 27.

13   'The Bristol Accord', EU Ministerial on Sustainable Communities, UK Presidency, Policy Papers, Office of the Deputy Prime Minister, March 2006.

14   Jones, P., Roberts M. and Morris, L., 2007, *op. cit.*

15   Department for Communities and Local Government. *National Planning Policy Framework*. CLG: London, March 2012, p. 17.

16   Department of the Environment, Transport and the Regions and the Commission for Architecture and the Built Environment, 2000, *op. cit.*

17   ibid.

18   CABE, 2004, *op. cit.*

19   Department of the Environment, Transport and the Regions and the Commission for Architecture and the Built Environment, 2000, *op. cit.*, p. 8.

20   Alexander, C., Neis, H., Anninou, A. and King, I., *A New Theory of Urban Design*. Oxford University Press: Oxford, 1987.

21   CABE, 2004, *op. cit.*, p. 13.

22   ibid.

23   Department for Communities and Local Government. *Preparing Design Codes: A practice manual*. CLG: London, November 2006, p. 10

24   ibid.

25   Campbell, K., *Massive Small: The operating programme for smart urbanism*. Urban Exchange: London, 2011, pp. 21–25.

26   Cowan, R., *The Dictionary of Urbanism*. Streetwise Press: Tisbury, 2005, p. 49.

27   Conzen, M. R. G., Morphogenesis and Structure of the Historic Townscape in Britain. In: Conzen, M. P. (ed.), *M.R.G. Conzen: Thinking about Urban Form. Papers on urban morphology, 1932–1998*. Peter Lang: Bern, 2004, pp. 60–61.

28   ibid., p. 75.

29   English Partnerships and the Housing Corporation, 2000, *op. cit.*, p. 67.

30   Department for Communities and Local Government, 2006, *op. cit.*

31   English Partnerships and the Housing Corporation, 2000, *op. cit.*, p. 64.

32   ibid.

33   Bürklin, T. and Peterek, M., *Urban Building Blocks*. Birkhäuser: Basel, 2008.

34   Department of the Environment, Heritage and Local Government, *Guidelines for Planning Authorities on Sustainable Residential Development in Urban Areas (Cities, Towns and Villages)*. Government of Ireland: Dublin, 2009. Available at: http://www.environ.ie/en/Publications/DevelopmentandHousing/Planning/FileDownLoad,19164,en.pdf, p. 67.

35   Department of the Environment, Transport and the Regions, *The Use of Density in Urban Planning*, 1998.

36   Department of the Environment, Heritage and Local Government, 2009, *op. cit.*, p. 67.

37   Department of the Environment, Transport and the Regions and the Commission for Architecture and the Built Environment, 2000, *op. cit.*

38   Local Government Boards for England, Wales and Scotland. *Report of the Committee appointed by the President of the Local Government Board and the Secretary for Scotland to consider questions of building construction in connection with the provision of dwellings for the working classes in England and Wales and Scotland, and report upon methods of securing economy and dispatch in the provision of such dwellings*, Stationery Office: London, 1918, p. 12. (Parliamentary Papers online copyright of Pro-quest information and learning company, 2006.)

39   Jacobs, J., 1961, *op. cit.*

40   ibid., p. 156.

41   NEF (New Economics Foundation), 2010, *op. cit.*

42   Cullingworth, B. and Nadin, V., *Town Planning in the UK* (14th edn). Routledge: Abingdon, 2006.

43   Cowan, R., 2005, *op. cit.*, p. 383.

44   EU Ministerial Informal on Sustainable Communities, UK Presidency, Office of the Deputy Prime Minister, March 2006.

45   Department for Communities and Local Government. *National Planning Policy Framework*. CLG: London, March 2012.

46   DEFRA. *Definition and Components of Sustainable Communities*, DEFRA: London, March, 2005.

47   Panerai, P., Castex, J., Depaule, J. C. and Samuels, I., *Urban Forms: The death and life of the urban block*. Architectural Press: Oxford, 2004, p. 166.

48   Whitelaw, I., *A Measure of all Things: The story of measurement through the ages*. David and Charles: Hove, 2007.

49   HATC, *Housing Space Standards*. Greater London Authority: London, 2006, p. 20.

50   Kostof, S., *The City Shaped: Urban patterns and meanings through history*. Thames and Hudson: London, 1991.

51   HC Deb 20 December 2010 cc143-5WS, quoted in, *Localism Bill*: Planning and Housing Bill 126 of 2010–11, RESEARCH PAPER 11/03, 11 January 2011.

52   Ministry of Housing, Spatial Planning and the Environment Communication Directorate, *Making Spaces, Sharing Space: Fifth National Policy on Spatial Planning, 2000/2020*, The Hague, 2001. Cited in Cousins, M., *Design Quality in New Housing: Learning from the Netherlands*. Taylor and Francis: Abingdon, 2009, pp.16–17.

53   Welsh Assembly Government, *Planning Policy Wales* (edition 4), 2011, p. 58. Available at: http://wales.gov.uk/docs/desh/publications/110228ppwedition4en.pdf

54   Welsh Assembly Government, *Planning Policy Wales Technical Advice Note 12: Design*, 2009. Available at: http://wales.gov.uk/docs/desh/publications/090807tan12en.pdf

55   Welsh Assembly Government, 2011, *op. cit.*, p. 51.

56   Scottish Government, *Scottish Planning Policy*, 2010. Available at: http://www.scotland.gov.uk/Publications/2010/02/03132605/0

57   Scottish Government, *Planning Advice Note 83: Masterplanning*, 2008. Available at: http://www.scotland.gov.uk/Resource/Doc/244134/0068213.pdf

58   Department of the Environment (NI), *Planning Policy Statement 1: General Principles*. Department of the Environment: Belfast, 1998, p. 11.

59   Department of the Environment, Heritage and Local Government, 2009, *op. cit.*

60   Department for Communities and Local Government. *Garden Developments: Understanding the issues – an investigation into residential development on gardens in England*. CLG, January 2010, p. 5.

61   Department for Communities and Local Government, 2012, *op. cit.*

62   http://www.designcouncil.org.uk/our-work/CABE/Localism-and-planning/Building-for-Life/

63   Department for Communities and Local Government, 2012, *op. cit.*, p. 15.

64   CABE, *What Home Buyers Want: Attitudes and decision making among consumers*. CABE: London, 2005, p. 1.

65   Department for Communities and Local Government, 2002, *op. cit.*

66   Prince's Foundation for the Built Environment, *Delivering Sustainable Urbanism: A strategic land investment model*, 2010, p. 4.

67   Department for Communities and Local Government, 2002, *op. cit.*

68   National Self Build Association, *Self Build as a Volume Housing Solution*. NaSBA, 2008, p. 9.

69   Savills Research, *Market in Minutes: UK residential development land*, October 2010. Available at: http://pdf.euro.savills.co.uk/uk/market-in-minute-reports/residential-development-land-oct-2010.pdf.

70   Prince's Foundation for the Built Environment, 2010, *op. cit.*, p. 5.

71   PlacesMatter!, *The Economic Value of Good Design*. PlacesMatter! and the Northwest Regional Development Agency: Liverpool, 2009.

72   Scottish Government, *Delivering Better Places in Scotland: A guide to learning from broader experience*, January 2011. Available at: http://www.scotland.gov.uk/ Publications/2010/12/31110906/0

73   Department for Communities and Local Government, 2002, *op. cit.*

74   CABE, 2005, *op. cit.*, p. 1.

75   Cousins, M., *Design Quality in New Housing: Learning from the Netherlands*. Taylor and Francis: Abingdon, 2009, pp. 43–44.

76   CABE, 2005, *op. cit.*

77   *The Times*, 'High street bargains? Try living above a shop', 2 April 2010.

78   Falk, N., *How the Dutch fund infrastructure: Lessons from Vathorst in Amersfoort*. Urbed (unpublished), 2010, p. 1.

79   Scottish Government, 2011, *op. cit.*

80   Ibid.

81   Department for Communities and Local Government. *The Community Infrastructure Levy: An overview*. CLG: London, May 2011.

82   *The Guardian (Society)*, 'Strong foundations', 6 July 2011.

83   The Heritage Council and Dublin City Council, *Built to Last: The sustainable reuse of buildings*. The Heritage Council and Dublin City Council: Dublin, 2004.

84   Smith, A., *An Inquiry into the Nature and Causes of the Wealth of Nations*. Harriman House: Hampshire, 5th edn, 1776, p. 548.

85   Department for Communities and Local Government, 2002, *op. cit.*

86   Klettner, A., *Riba urges architects to get involved with localism*. Article published by bdonline.co.uk, 15 December 2010. Available at: http://m.bdonline. co.uk/news/riba-urges-architects-to-get-involved-with-localism/5010411.article

87   Collins, J. and Moren, P., *Good Practice Guide: Negotiating the Planning Maze*, RIBA Publishing: London, 3rd edn, 2009, p. 61.

88   CABE, *The Use of Urban Design Codes: Building Sustainable Communities*. CABE: London, undated.

89   This latter point doesn't apply in the Republic of Ireland because development control is already a function of the executive, not the elected members.

90   Local Government Group and the Planning Advisory Service, *LDOs and Localism: Can Local Development Orders contribute to the new planning agenda?* Local Government Group: London, 2011.

91   Prince's Foundation for the Built Environment, 2010, *op. cit.*

92   National Self Build Association, 2008, *op. cit.*, p. 8.

93   Department for Communities and Local Government. *Laying the foundations: A Housing Strategy for England*. HM Government, November 2011. p. 15.

94   http://webarchive.nationalarchives.gov. uk/20110118095356/http://www.cabe.org.uk/ case-studies/vauban

95   Scottish Government, 2011, *op. cit.*

96   http://www.vauban.de

97   http://www.cohousing.org.uk

98   Scottish Government, 2011, *op. cit.*

99   Gemeente Almere, 2010. *Homeruskwartier Centrum: Zelf Bouwen*. Municipality of Almere. Available at: http://www. homeruskwartier-centrum.nl/

100 Scottish Government, 2011, *op.cit.*

101 ibid.

102 In conversation with Annica Carlsson, Managing Director of Equator Architects, Stockholm, and, separately, with officers of the Stockholm City Planning Department.

103 Ministère de l'Équipement, *Guide des zones d'aménagement concertés*, La Documentation française, 1989.

104 Tübingen Municipal Office for Revitalisation, Tübingen: Südstadt Development Städtebaulicher

Entwicklungsbereich 'Stuttgarter Straße / Französisches Viertel', Tübingen/Germany (unpublished), 2005.

105 Campbell, K., 2011, *op. cit.*, p. 82.

106 Keedwell, P., 'Psychitecture'. Available at: http://www.drkeedwell.com/drkeedwell/%22Psychitecture%22.html

107 Barton, H., Grant, M. and Guise, R., *Shaping Neighbourhoods for Local Health and Global Sustainability*, Routledge: Abingdon, 2nd edn, 2010. p. 243.

108 Campbell, K., 2011, *op. cit.*, p. 98.

109 Department for Communities and Local Government, 2012, *op. cit.*, p. 13.

110 Urban Task Force,1999, *op. cit.*

111 Barton, H., Grant, M. and Guise, R., 2010, *op. cit.*

112 Urban Task Force, 1999, *op. cit.*

113 Barton, H., Grant, M. and Guise, R., 2010, *op. cit.*

114 Levitt, D., *The Housing Design Handbook*: *A guide to good practice*. Routledge: Oxford, 2010, p. 38.

115 ibid., p. 92.

116 Office of the Deputy Prime Minister, *Safer Places: The planning system and crime prevention*. OPDM: London, 2004. Available at http://www.securedbydesign.com/pdfs/safer_places.pdf

117 London Development Agency, *London Housing Design Guide (interim edition)*. LDA: London, 2010. Available at: http://www.designforlondon.gov.uk/uploads/media/Interim_London_Housing_Design_Guide.pdf

118 London Plan, 2011, p. 87–88. Available at: http://www.london.gov.uk/sites/default/files/The%20London%20Plan%202011.pdf

119 Levitt, D., 2010, *op. cit.*

120 See TRADA. Eurocode 5 span tables.

121 Cowan, R., 2005, *op. cit.*, p. 407.

122 Office of the Deputy Prime Minister, 2004, *op. cit.*

123 McCullogh, N., *Dublin: An urban history – the plan of the city*. Anne Street Press in association with the Lilliput Press: Dublin, 2007, p. 191.

124 See Levitt (2010) for more detailed versions of 'generic' house plans, which, in turn, can trace their evolution to 'preferred dwelling plans' published by the former Greater London Council (GLC) in 1977.

125 Imrie, R., *Accessible Housing: Quality, disability and design*. Routledge: London, 2006, p. 132.

126 CABE, 2004, *op. cit.*, p. 93.

127 CABE, undated, *op. cit.*

128 Campbell, K., 2011, *op. cit.*, p. 52.

129 Department for Communities and Local Government, 2011, *op. cit.*, p. 33.

130 CABE, undated, *op. cit.*, p. 5.

131 The *bebauungspläne* translates more closely as 'development plan' or 'construction plan', however in the German context it is sufficiently versatile to be used to define plots as well.

132 Owen, S. (Department for Communities and Local Government), *Lessons from International Self Build Housing Practices*. Prepared for the National Self Build Association (NaSBA) on behalf of the joint Government-Industry Self Build Working Group, 2011, p. 27. Available at: www.nasba.org.uk/Content/Reports.aspx

133 Department for Transport, *Manual for Streets*. Thomas Telford Publishing: London, 2007.

134 Office of the Deputy Prime Minister, 2004, *op. cit.*

135 English Partnerships and the Housing Corporation, *op. cit.*, 2000, p. 87.

136 Department for Transport, 2007, *op. cit.* Note that the *Manual for Streets* was supplemented by a companion volume in 2010 covering the design of mixed-use streets.

137 The Building Regulations, 2010, give effect to the 2004 edition of Approved Document M.

138 Levitt, D., 2010, *op. cit.*

139 Essex County Council, *Essex Design* Guide, 2005. Available at: http://www.the-edi.co.uk/downloads/19715_essexdesignguide.pdf

140 Department of the Environment (NI), *Creating Places: Achieving quality in residential developments*:

incorporating guidance on layout and access. DoE: Belfast, 2000, p. 52.

141   CABE, 2005, *op. cit.*, p. 16.

142   Royal Institute of British Architects, *The Case for Space: The size of England's new homes.* RIBA: London, 2010, p. 9.

143   Littlefair, P. J., *Site layout planning for sunlight and daylight: a guide to good practice.* Building Research Establishment: Watford, 1991, p. 5.

144   Department for Communities and Local Government. *The Party Wall etc. Act 1996: An explanatory booklet.* CLG, 2002.

145   Waite, R., Urban Splash to replace Tutti Frutti with modular family homes. *Architect's Journal*, 235 (10), 2011, p. 9.

index